Ancient Civilizations

A Captivating Guide to Mayan History, the Aztecs, and Inca Empire

Created by

Contents

Free Bonus from Captivating History (Available for a Limited time)

Hi History Lovers!

Now you have a chance to join our exclusive history list so you can get your first history ebook for free as well as discounts and a potential to get more history books for free! Simply visit the link below to join.

Captivatinghistory.com/ebook

Also, make sure to follow us on:

Twitter: @Captivhistory

Facebook: Captivating History: @captivatinghistory

Part 1: Maya Civilization

A Captivating Guide to Maya History and Maya Mythology

Introduction

You've probably heard of the Maya and their astounding civilization before. You may recognize the famous Maya calendar that apparently predicted a worldwide apocalypse back in 2012. The media were quick to jump on board this mind-boggling prophecy (which we'll debunk later in this book). Newspapers and websites were filled with stories of doomsday that failed to materialize. Lucky for us, we did wake up on December 22, 2012, when the Maya calendar apparently ended.

But what you may not know is how much the Maya legacy is impacting your life today. Do you love to treat yourself to a frothy hot chocolate before bed, or indulge in an after-dinner chocolate treat? Do you love adding a side of fries to your meal? What about tomatoes for your favorite Italian dishes? If you do, you may not be aware that you have the Maya and the Spanish conquistadors to thank, for they introduced these goods to Europe and other continents.

But Maya are far more than just their food. In this captivating guide, you'll discover why Maya have gained such worldwide admiration over the many other civilizations that existed in Mesoamerica at the time. You'll learn how the Maya civilization developed, the major turning points in their 3,000-year-long history, the mysteries surrounding their demise, and some of the unique places where Maya exist to this day.

Oh yes. If you think the Maya are gone, think again. As opposed to popular belief, the Maya are neither extinct, nor quiet. They are six-million strong, according to some sources, most of them living in Guatemala. What's more, in 1994 one of the surviving Maya tribes, the Zapatistas, launched a rebellion in southeast Mexico against global trade and capitalism.

In the first part of this book, we'll first examine the origins of the Maya civilization and the Mesoamerican cultures that may have influenced them. We'll discuss why Maya (out of all the different tribes that existed in the region at the time) have captured the imagination of the West so much. We'll look at how they lived, ate, slept, whom they worshipped, and how they used herbal medicines and hallucinogenic plants to treat the sick.

We'll look at their trading routes and rivalries with another famous Mesoamerican tribe—the Aztecs. We'll look into the decline of the Maya civilization and how their rivalries with the Aztecs aided the victory of the Spanish conquistadors in the 16th century, led by the famous Spaniard Hernán Cortés. We won't forget to mention the heroic efforts of the Maya to fend off the Spaniards, and why they were able to succeed at this task for much longer than the Aztecs. We'll even track down the Maya living today, a population that is still six-million strong and adhere to many of the traditions that their ancestors once held. In among the battle tales and gore of human sacrifice, we'll look at some delicious cocoa recipes, Maya-style, that you can make at home.

After we've learnt all about the Maya origins, their cuisine, and their most notable events to present day, we'll delve into the aspect that's often the reason why so many people have been fascinated by the Maya civilization throughout the ages. We will look at their mythology, cosmology, and the solar calendar that resulted in the infamous doomsday scare back in 2012.

So buckle up and get ready to be transported to the warm and wet plains of the Maya civilization—it will be a journey you'll never forget.

Maya Timeline

The Archaic Period:
- 7000 to 2000 BC

The Preclassic Period:
- Early Preclassic – 2000 to 1000 BC
- Middle Preclassic – 1000 to 300 BC
- Late Preclassic – 300 BC to AD 250

The Classic Period:
- Early Classic – AD 250 to 600
- Late Classic – AD 600 to 900
- Terminal Classic – AD 900 to 1000

The Postclassic Period:
- Early Postclassic – AD 1000 to 1250
- Late Postclassic – AD 1250 to 1521
- The Spanish Invasion – AD 1521

Glossary of Important Maya Terms

- Cacao – the seeds that the Maya used in order to create their delicious cacao drink, also known as "bitter water."
- Cenote – a type of sink-hole that the Maya used to get fresh supplies of water (and to perform ritual sacrifice).
- Conquistadors – the Spanish military leaders who led the conquest of America in the 16th century, including Hernándo Cortés.

- The Dresden Codex – located in a museum in Germany, the Dresden Codex is one of the oldest surviving books from the Americas. It contains 78 pages with important information on rituals, calculations, and the planetary movements of Venus.
- Haab – one of the several Maya calendars (this one measured time in 365-day cycles).
- Hero Twins – the central characters in the Maya creation story and the ancestors of future Maya rulers.
- Huipil – traditional dress for Maya women.
- Maize – the staple food of Maya civilization, an ancient form of corn (the Maize god was one of the most important deities for Maya).
- Mesoamerica – this is what we call the region of the Americas before the arrival of the Spanish fleets and its colonisation in the 15th and 16th centuries.
- Popol Vuh – the story of creation of the world that was passed down from generation to generation (it was recorded by the Quiche Maya who lived in the region of modern day Guatemala).
- Shamanism – an important spiritual practice throughout Mesoamerica (during shamanic trance a shaman would be able to practice divination and healing).
- Stelae – an upright stone slab or column, often used as a gravestone. These structures usually contained commemorative inscriptions.
- Yucatan Peninsula – a region in the southeast of Mexico, where some of the Maya civilization developed, especially in the Postclassic period.

Part 1 – History

Chapter 1: The Origins of the Mesoamerican Civilizations

Maya have captivated the imagination of the West ever since their culture was "discovered" in the 1840s by the American writer and explorer John Lloyd Stephens and the English artist and architect Frederick Catherwood. The latter is best known for his intricate and detailed images of the Maya ruins that he and Stephens later published in their book *Incidents of Travel in Central America*.

But just because the West didn't discover the Maya until the mid-nineteenth century doesn't mean that they lived in obscurity the rest of the time. In fact, their history is rich with fantastical tales and splendour and a diet that people living in other regions at the time could only dream about. The origins of the Maya civilization can be traced all the way back to 7,000 BC.

The Archaic period: 7000 – 2000 BC

People were once hunter-gatherers, living a largely nomadic lifestyle, according to the whims of nature and the sharp-toothed animals all around them. They had to keep moving in order to stay safe and keep up their food supplies. But in 7000 BC a new shift began—the hunter-gatherers who lived in Mesoamerica discovered something that would change their region forever. They began planting crops.

It's not entirely clear why this shift occurred when it did. The changing weather patterns may have had something to do with it—the climate gradually became wetter and warmer, so many of the larger animals that the Mesoamericans relied on for food became extinct. As a result, they had to eat more plants and grains, so eventually they started growing some for themselves. They used many techniques to make their lands more fertile. For example, they discovered that burning trees helped put nitrates into the soil to make it more fertile. (Don't try this at home.)

As a result, these ancient people started having a much more varied diet. We know this thanks to the discoveries by the archaeologists working in the Tehuacan Valley of Mexico, a site that contains the best evidence for human activity in the Archaic time period in Mesoamerica. The locals were able to plant and eat things that we often take for granted today, such as peppers, squash, and avocado. Not to mention early forms of corn, the grain that would become the staple food in Mesoamerica.

Since they were able to grow the food that they needed in order to survive, these ancient people no longer needed to move around as much. They began settling down into small villages, leading to the first known settlements in Mesoamerica. The first evidence of individual burial spots directly under people's homes dates back to 2600 BC. These early settlements included temples and sacred spots for worship, suggesting an early form of a civilization. Temples, worship, and sacrifice remained a prominent theme throughout the Maya history, and we'll cover more of it later.

But the Maya did not evolve in a vacuum. There were many cultures and tribes that existed around them, and each had some influence on their culture, customs, and civilization. We'll examine these, one at a time, as we travel through time to really appreciate the interplay between those cultures and the Maya. Before we go onto learning about how these early settlements evolved into the Maya civilization, let's look at one of the most important tribes that existed in Mesoamerica at the time—the Olmecs.

The Olmecs: 1,200 – 300 BC

No one really knows where the Olmecs came from or where they disappeared to. But their legacy on the Mesoamerican tribes, including the Maya, is huge.

The Olmecs inhabited the area along the Gulf of Mexico, and their impressive stone cities gave way to myths about giants who may have lived in this area at the time. The Olmec craftsmanship was highly sophisticated—there are some impressive sculptures that survive to this day as evidence of their superb skills.

Sometimes ancient history is a bit of guesswork, leaving you to fill in the gaps left out by missing evidence. It's interesting that there's a total lack of battle scenes in the Olmec art—something that most other cultures are quick to display in their monuments and sculptures. The fact that they depict no battle scenes could mean one of two things. Either they did not engage in any war conflict, or they simply didn't feel like showing off about it. You decide.

Until recently, the Olmecs were regarded as the "mother culture" of all the great Mesoamerican civilizations to come, including the Maya and the Aztecs. But more recent sources argue that the Maya actually had a counter-influence on the Olmecs.

When it comes to the Olmec mythology, displayed in their surviving temples and sculptures, there are definite traces of shamanic practice. Many of their sculptures depict a were-jaguar, a core element of shamanism, symbolizing shamanic trance. The Maya saw the jaguar as a transformational animal, who feels at home at night-time, a symbol for the Underworld. The symbolism of shamanistic practice is present in all later Mesoamerican cultures, including the Maya.

The Olmecs may have had an important motif of a twin deity, that may have influenced the mythology of the Maya Hero Twins. The Hero Twins is a way to express the duality that the Maya saw around them—the complementary duality between day and night, life and death, the masculine and the feminine. The Olmec flaming eyebrows, the first corn, and cross bands are all symbols that would later appear in the Maya art, connected to astrology. Ancestor worship was also prevalent in the Olmec tradition, as it was later in the Maya and most Mesoamerican cultures at the time.

Challenge your perceptions—Dwarfism

When studying ancient history and learning about cultures, it's always interesting to find out what light it can shed on the culture that we inhabit today. Sometimes the things that we perceive as true are to do with our cultural upbringing. For example, nowadays we define people who are born with smaller organisms and don't grow much taller than 147cm as having the medical condition of Dwarfism or "short stature." We tend to see this as an abnormality, assuming that people born with this condition would face certain limitations in life.

Well, the Olmec also saw Dwarfism as an abnormality, only not a limiting one. In fact, it was quite the opposite. As the director of the Maya Exploration Center, Dr. Edwin Barnhart explains in his audio-lecture series *Maya To Aztec: Ancient Mesoamerica Revealed* that if you were born with a very small organism in the Olmec or the later Maya culture, you'd be seen as a magical being, touched by the gods. You'd be enjoying all kinds of luxuries, often appearing in the king's court. This may be something to do with their belief that the sky was held up by four dwarves, and so they gave them special treatment.

Chapter 2: The Preclassic Period and the Magnificent Zapotec

The Preclassic period has quite a timespan—starting in 2000 BC and finishing in AD 250, this time period covers a history of more than two millennia. That's quite a stretch to fit into a single chapter, but let's try and sum up the most important and interesting tales from that era. For convenience, archaeologists break down this long-time period into the Early, Middle, and Late Preclassic.

Early Preclassic period: 2000 to 1000 BC

This period marks the beginning of agriculture for the Maya. We already discussed how agriculture led to the first settlements but it's in the Early Preclassic period that we see them really advancing. For examples, ceramics and household architecture were developed and used in the Maya communities in the Early Preclassic period. How did the Maya people live at this time? The Maya were family-centered. There was not much of a social hierarchy (that came later). Maya were largely farmers, growing domesticated crops, such as maize, all kinds of exotic fruits, cacao, and root crops. But their diet (one of the healthiest diets you could have in the ancient world) still depended largely on hunting and fishing in the lush fields and waters that surrounded them.

Cuello and early Maya architecture

The earliest evidence of Maya architecture can be found in northern Belize, on a site named Cuello. This is an incredibly important site for exploring how the early Maya lived. It emerged sometime around 1000 BC. While Cuello was by no means the only village in the vicinity, it's certainly the largest, boasting a population of 2,600 in these early times. The early structures from Cuello had thin plaster floors, built on top of a low platform made of small black stones and clay. There was possibly a wooden superstructure also.

Frank and Julie Saul have studied the remnants at Cuello—their findings have sparked some fascinating insights into how the Maya lived. They couldn't find many burials of people older than 55 – 59 years on the site, suggesting that the average lifespan of a Maya was rarely, if ever, more than that. They also excavated at least five individuals with healed fractures, a display of the Maya healing practices at the time. One particular find was a male, aged between 55 and 59, who had suffered from arthritis and severe dental problems. His skeleton showed a healed fracture. Examining his skeleton closer led Frank and Julie to conclude that he may have incurred his fracture while holding a shield in combat. He didn't have an individual grave—he was buried in a mass grave of 32 adults (only one of them was female). Other mass graves excavated in the area share a similar story, showing the dominance of the male culture.

Middle Preclassic period: 1000 to 300 BC

This period marks a rapid expansion of the Maya across the lowlands. Their villages grew both in size and population. As they did so, the social structures changed, becoming more complex and hierarchical. There was also more contact with other Mesoamerican cultures, including the Olmec.

One such evidence comes from the great city of Chiapa de Corzo that was inhabited as early as 1200 BC. Site excavations have found the burial site of an important person, perhaps even a ruler, whose grave was embellished with 3000 artefacts from all over Mesoamerica, spreading far and wide from modern Mexico to Honduras. Chiapa de Corzo's architecture shows an Olmec influence. Archaeologists believe that the city had close ties with the important Olmec center called La Venta.

Between 700 and 500 BC, Chiapa de Corzo became an important structural town, consisting of complex buildings. Public monumental buildings were made of clay and carefully arranged into the city's plan. The public ceremonial precinct covered 20 of the total 70 hectares of Chiapa de Corzo. A massive depositing of ritual axes has been found in front of an astronomical building, suggesting the importance of ritual and worship in this early Maya society.

Fairly recently a tomb of a great Maya king was discovered at a temple site in Retalhuleu province in modern Guatemala. Archaeologists place it somewhere between 700 and 400 BC. It is known as the Tomb of the Vulture Lord because the skeleton of the male buried in this tomb was clad in rich jade jewels with a necklace of a vulture-headed human figure tied around his neck. The vulture would later become an important symbol for the Maya, indicating a ruler with power and influential economic status. The government archaeologist Miguel Orrego commented that K'utz Chman (or Grandfather Vulture in the Mayan language) was a big chief, who probably bridged the gap between the Olmec and Maya cultures in central America.

As well as the Olmec, Maya developed vast networks with other villages and settlements in the area. One of their trading partners and influences was the civilization known as the Zapotec.

The Zapotec: 600 BC to AD 800

Known also as the "Cloud People," the Zapotec lived in the southern highlands of Central Mesoamerica. They had extensive trade and cultural ties with the Olmec, Maya, and another civilization that existed in Mesoamerica at the time, the Teotihuacan. Thanks to their early ties with the Olmec, the Zapotec were able to construct their great city of Monte Albán. This enabled the Zapotec to become the most influential force of the region throughout the Classic period. They built at least 15 other palaces in the surrounding valleys of Oaxaca. One of their great cities, Mitla, would become the most important city for the Zapotec around AD 900, containing plazas decorated with rich reliefs and geometric designs.

We'll get into the Late Preclassic period in just a moment, but it's worth mentioning here that by the Late Preclassic period the Zapotec cities showed remarkable achievements and sophistication in important spheres, such as the arts, architecture, writing, and engineering (for instance, the advanced irrigation systems). The Zapotec were a highly sophisticated and rich culture. And not only that, the Zapotec also developed detailed ideas of astronomy and mathematics, and a calendar that arguably lay the blueprint for the Maya calendar.

The Zapotec not only loved their inventions—they loved their sports, too. Excavations of a large stone-faced platform in the site called Dainzu shows reliefs of players engaged in the game that was played all over Mesoamerica at the time—the Ball Game. But it's quite different from modern football—it was a game entwined with religious practice, and sometimes played to life and death. We'll look at the rules of the game in more detail in a later chapter.

Late Preclassic period: 300 BC to AD 250

This is the time period that saw the rise of two powerful states: Kaminaljuyu in the highlands and El Mirador in the lowlands. Kaminaljuyu was the largest of all highland cities, growing cotton and corn on a scale that had never been seen before. The state was built in a fertile valley, encompassing a lake and surrounded by volcanoes. Obsidian was mined and crafted in this great city, and traded to cities and villages far, far away. The city's architecture shows its thirst for more and more power. It depicts scenes of captives, naked and bound, wearing impressive headdresses that were symbolic of rulers. Kaminaljuyu now forms the foundation of the modern Guatemala City, and much of it remains buried beneath this city.

Although it rose to power in the Late Preclassic period, Kaminaljuyu was actually inhabited as early as 1500 BC and saw its demise only in AD 1200. That's almost 3000 years of history in a single city—arguably much longer than our current civilization!

Chapter 3: The Classic Period, Doomsday Calendar, and the Mystery of the Red Queen

Let's travel forward to the time period that architects refer to as the Classic period. This is when the Maya really thrived, with many remarkable accomplishments, including the development of their calendar, polychrome ceramics, huge ball courts, and their famous pyramids. The Maya thrived in all aspects, enjoying tremendous developments and a steady increase in population.

This period is broken down into three parts: the Early, Late and Terminal Classic period. This is a fascinating time in the Maya history, containing mysteries that puzzle historians and archaeologists to this day. These include the sophisticated Maya calendar and the Tomb of the Red Queen, arguably the only Maya female ruler.

Early Classic – AD 250 to 600

Belize was an important area, containing almost one million inhabitants by AD 600, according to some sources. The Maya had become experts at agriculture by this time; for example, they used stone-walled terraces (some as tall as six feet and 100 yards in length). In order to control water levels during rainy season, the Maya dug a number of ditches in the area.

Until this time, there were few monuments found in the Maya-inhabited Mesoamerica. The Classic period is when we see an organized calendar system emerge, which helped to date many of the monuments or stelae. These also recorded the political, social, and religious history of the Maya.

How Maya measured the time

The Maya calendar has been known for some time as one of the most accurate tools to measure time in the entire human history. Can you imagine how skilled their mathematicians and astronomers were to rival our modern devices? But they didn't just have one calendar—they had a calendar measuring one solar year (called the Haab), a sacred calendar that represented the nine cycles of the Moon (called the Tzolk'in), and a calendar for any events spanning over 52 years (called the Long Count).

The Haab measured one solar year in 365 days. But unlike our 12-month calendars, the Haab measured time in 18 months, each consisting of 20 days. It also had an additional 19th month that was only five days long! Altogether, this 19-month cycle forms 365 days. To this day, the remaining Maya farmers (yes, there are still plenty of them around!) in the Yucatan region perform special rites and rituals surrounding this calendar. We'll look at those in a later chapter.

By interweaving the Haab and the Tzolk'in calendars, it is possible to make a Calendar Round that will produce a combination that will not occur again for 52 years. This is why elders who had reached 52 years of age were treated with special respect in the Maya civilization. The Maya saw life as a continuum of cycles of creation and destruction that occurred every 52 years. If humans neglected their responsibility to the gods, then a cycle of destruction would mark the next 52 years. This is why ritual sacrifice was so important for the Maya.

The Long Count calendar was reserved for mythical events spanning over 52 years. Counting days in a chronological order, the calendar began on August 11, 3114 BC that Maya believed to be the mythological day of creation. On December 21, 2012, the calendar completed a full cycle, reaching the same point as the creation. Mass media were quick to turn this into a fear-based story of sensational proportion, predicting a worldwide apocalypse. What's more likely though is that the calendar marked a new cycle for humankind, a kind of rebirth. Some of the Maya monuments predict that the world will continue for thousands of years to come.

The Maya also used their calendars for another purpose. Each day in the Maya calendar corresponded to a name. The Maya named their children according to the day they were born. Some examples of typical Maya names of that time include "Earthquake 1" and "Rainbow goddess."

Late Classic – AD 600 to 900

Of course, the increase in population meant that resources were becoming more and more scarce. This led to increased competition, conflict, and warfare. Many of the stelae and lintels found in the Maya lowlands display scenes of captives and violence, especially those found in Caracol, Tikal, and Naranjo. What happened to the captives of the Maya? They were used as slaves who had to construct buildings and perform public works. Some of them were sacrificed to Maya gods in special rituals and ceremonies. Either way, their fate was pretty grim.

The mystery of the Red Queen

The tomb of the so-called Maya Red Queen dates back from AD 600 to 700. It was discovered in 1994 by the Mexican archaeologist Arnoldo Gonzalez Cruz inside Temple XIII in the ruins of the ancient Maya city of Palenque.

But why the color red? Well, red was an important color for the Maya. They saw all buildings as living entities, and so they painted their pyramids, ball courts, and other important buildings in red.

And who was the mysterious Red Queen? It took ages to get to the tomb and open the sarcophagus, but it was all worth it in the end. Inside the coffin was a noblewoman, clad in red cinnabar powder, along with the many objects that were to accompany her on her journey into afterlife. There was an impressive collection of pearls, jade, shells, and bone needles. The woman's face was covered with a special mask made of malachite pieces; her skull was covered with a diadem made of flat circular jade beads. A man who is thought to be her servant was discovered in the same tomb—it was customary for the Maya servants to accompany their masters in the afterlife.

After her skeleton was transported to a laboratory, carbon 14 tests revealed that she had osteoporosis but she'd lived to the grand age of sixty. Her diet was mostly meat-based and she had incredibly healthy teeth for an ancient Maya. Although no inscriptions were found inside the tomb that would reveal her name, Cruz believes that she was Tz'ak-bu Ajaw, the grandmother of the last Maya king. And since only 10% of the great ancient city of Palenque has been explored so far, it gives hope that one day we'll be able to find out who the Red Queen was.

Terminal Classic – AD 900 to 1000

As opposed to the thriving population and architecture of the Classic period, the Terminal Classic marks the decline of the Maya civilization. There is little or no evidence of major architectural works, possibly due to the rapidly declining population numbers. People abandoned the Maya cities, and the causes for this are unknown to this day. Of course, this is fertile soil for theories and debates to find a cause for this decline. Just like the extinction of the dinosaurs, the end of the Maya civilization is a question that has captured the imagination of dozens of historians. Their proposed theories are usually divided into two camps: external and internal factors.

External factors

Foreign invasion from the west is one of the more popular theories, based on the ideas that foreign invaders may have disrupted the Maya society to such an extent that it led to its decline. Theorists who support this idea propose that Mexican-related cultures (such as the Putun Maya from Tabasco) may have been to blame. However, evidence for such theories is somewhat scarce—only a few sites along the Usumacinta River (like Seibal and Altar de Sacrificios) carry signs of a foreign invasion of that degree.

Changes in trade is another popular theory that has been put forward over the years. It suggests that there was a major change in trade networks at the beginning of this era. Overland trade routes were swapped to maritime trade routes, and so large and landlocked cities (such as the aforementioned grand cities of Tikal, Caracol, and Calakmul) were bypassed. Thus, they were no longer as important, leading to a collapse of their economy.

Internal factors

Social upheaval was a popular theory for many years, first put forward by Sir Eric Thompson over 50 years ago. He argued that the oppressed lower Maya classes may have risen up against their elite leaders. This could have led to anarchy and a disruption in the Maya social order, but today only a few archaeologists continue to support this idea.

Natural catastrophes is one of the theories put forward to explain the collapse of the Maya civilization during this time period. These include earthquakes, volcanic eruptions, and epidemics, among others. However, there is little geological evidence for this.
What could be more plausible though is ecological problems, such as prolonged drought. The growing population meant that there were more mouths to feed, and so more wood and other resources were required to create adequate supply of food. This meant that ancient land needed to be cleared for food production. But clearing out too much of the rainforest leads to changes in climate that could have resulted in long periods of drought, malnutrition, and eventually driven people to leave the major cities. Science seems to confirm this theory—studies of lake sediments in the southern Yucatan, Belize, and the Peten show evidence of long periods of very dry weather in AD 900, coinciding with the Terminal Classic period.

It's important to note though that not all Maya cities suffered the same fate. In fact, many continued to thrive, especially those by the riverbank. The cities that continued to thrive include Baking Pot and Cayo District. Tipu, Lamanai, and Santa Rita remained as important cities that kept good connections with the more northern cities. They would later play an important role in dealings with the Spanish conquistadors.

Chapter 4: Food, Rites, and Gruesome Tales

Before we go on and examine the next period in the Maya history, let's give them a chance to thrive a little longer. Let's take a step back and look at their foods, rites, and rituals—much of this is what they're known for today. We'll also look at how the Maya liked their hot chocolate—a recipe that you can try at home.

Maya food quiz

Remember we talked about the foods that Maya are known for to this day in the introduction of this book? Let's test your knowledge—fill in the gaps to find out all the foods that the Maya introduced to Europe.

1. A _ _ _ _ _ o
2. C _ _ _ i
3. C _ _ _ _ _ _ _ e
4. C _ _ _ _ e
5. C _ _ n
6. P _ _ _ _ a
7. S _ _ _ _ h
8. S _ _ _ t P _ _ _ _ _ _ s
9. T _ _ _ _ _ _ s*

*See Endnotes for answers

How many did you guess? And how many of these surprised you? It wasn't just corn and veg that the Maya ate—they consumed a lot of meat, too. Using tapas and spears, and later bows and arrows, they hunted only as much as they needed to consume. Their game included turkeys, curassows, wild boar, deer, and freshwater fish. They also didn't say no to a bit of turtle meat or insects. There's even archaeological evidence found of roasted iguanas. There's also evidence of

---

the Maya having eaten other more exotic animals, such as armadillos, tapirs, monkeys, and manatee.

The Maya were also beekeepers, sweetening their maize drinks with honey. Their cacao drink, the ancestor of hot chocolate, may have only been served during important ceremonies and feasts, although the evidence on that is inconclusive. The cacao bean was certainly valuable among the Maya, being used as currency instead of gold or silver which they actually saw as pretty worthless.

Despite the many foods that the Maya developed and consumed, they were not the ones to introduce bananas to Europe. This is a common misconception—bananas actually originated in Southeast Asia. Another misconception is that chilies originated in Asia. They did not. We know many types of chili today, grown all over the world, but the original came from Mesoamerica. Mexicans still have an interesting dish—a type of chili dish where they mix different types of beans, corn, and chili plants with chocolate. That's Maya heritage right there. And here's a recipe you can try at home for yourself.

How to make Maya hot chocolate at home

We love Maya for the gift of chocolate that they bestowed upon the world, developed sometime in AD 900. But the Maya didn't like it too sweet, as we do today. Their hot cacao drink was made of crushed cocoa beans, chili peppers and hot water. In fact, the word "chocolate" is believed to have come from the Maya "xocolatl" that literally means "bitter water." Nonetheless, it was seen as the "food of the gods," and Maya art often portrayed their gods enjoying a cup of the "bitter water."

If you still want to try some "bitter water" at home, here's how you can do it. Ideally, you'd have access to fresh cacao pods, and you'd ferment and dry them after picking them off the stalks, then roast them on a griddle. After that you'd take the shells off and grind the remaining seeds into a fine paste. But let's skip these steps, since we have the luxury of supermarkets. So step one is to go to a supermarket and buy a cacao mix—with no added ingredients, like sugar or dried milk powder. The more bitter the mix is, the better.

Now, mix the cacao powder with a little water until it forms a fine paste. Add some chili peppers to the mix, as well as some cornmeal or cornflour or maize powder (whatever you can find in a supermarket). Add some water and mix it all together. When your concoction is in a fairly liquid form, pour it back and forth from pot to cup, to pot, until you can see some froth forming on top. That's a sign that your Maya cacao drink is ready to be served. Enjoy!

How did the Maya grow their food?

Maya were early scientists, for they discovered quickly that a trio of vegetables that later became known as "the three sisters" grew very well together. These are squash, beans, and corn (sometimes called maize), the staple foods of the Maya civilization. The Maya found that these three plants, when grown together, would help each other develop. Tall and viny, beans climbed up the maize stalks. The squash, in turn, helped to reduce soil erosion.

There were many other foods that the Maya grew, using special agricultural techniques. And not only that. Food supplies were so important in Mesoamerica that the Maya had special religious rites and deities to honor. Here are some of them. The deities were so important that many religious rites were developed around the agricultural seasons.

The Maize god

Yes, corn was so important that it even had its own deity! Not only that—he was one of the most important deities in the Maya pantheon of gods (they had one for wind, one for rain, etc.). He was often portrayed with a head in the form of an ear of maize. He would even appear as the Creator god in Maya mythology—he was that important! The Maya religious text Popol Vuh describes the ancestors of humankind as having been made of maize.

The Maya beauty standards

For all their scientific and architectural accomplishments, the Maya did have some gruesome traditions. One such tradition shows just how important corn was to them. Born generally smaller than us, with dark skin, dark eyes, and straight black hair, the Maya did not pride their authentic look as a standard of beauty. They wanted to look like their Maize god, a deity that we'll get to know a bit better in the second part of this book, when we look at the Maya creation story. For now, let's just say that the Maize god was an incredibly important deity for the Maya, since their livelihood depended on their corn harvest. So the Maya wanted to have the same sloping forehead that their Maize god did, arguably resembling an ear of corn.

You may think that people in the Western world go to some extremes to aspire to the beauty archetypes we see in magazines today. But spending hours roasting your skin in the tanning studio, following some pretty whacky diets, or even injecting Botox is nothing compared to the Maya efforts to look like their Maize god.

And they started early on. Whether you were a priest, a bricklayer, a farmer, or even a slave, when a baby was born into your household, you began shaping him or her to honor the Maize god. For a good few days, the Maya would bind their newborn's head between two boards. They'd increase the pressure gradually, so that the head would mold and eventually the child would develop a deeply sloped forehead. It didn't matter if an infant died as part of this process—the sloped head was just too damn attractive.

If the infant did survive and developed the prized sloped head, it is believed that it didn't affect their intelligence much, as the brain is incredibly plastic in newborns and was able to mold to the new shape. But a child who'd survived the "corn treatment" was in for another surprise. Maya were also attracted to anyone who had crossed eyes. So the parents would dangle a piece of carrot or resin on some string in front of the baby's eyes, causing them to focus on it and for the eyes to rotate inward.

Pointed teeth were also highly esteemed in the Maya society, especially among women. Without any painkillers, they would file their teeth to achieve a sharp edge or a T-shape. Some would also decorate their teeth with plaques of pyrite, jade, or obsidian. They also pierced their nose, ears, and lips with jewellery made from jade, steel, and wood. Among men, it was common practice to tattoo their bodies with ink and scars.

While their bodies were important, clothes not so much, except for the headdresses. The grander your headdress, the higher your status in society, and you'd only wear these at grand ceremonies or special events, such as the Ball Game matches.

The sacred Ball Game

Apart from food, Maya also came up with some pretty amazing inventions that we still use to this day. For example, a screw top lid and rubber, the same one we use on our car tyres today. In fact, according to some studies, the Maya rubber was just as stable as Goodyear tyres. To get the right consistency, Maya harvested latex from their rubber trees, then mixed it with juice that they got from the vines of a plant called "morning glory." They discovered that these vines contained a special chemical that made the latex less brittle once it solidified.

Rubber became an incredibly important resource not only for Maya, but for most of the Mesoamerican cultures. Just like we celebrate the best footballers today, the ancient Mesoamericans celebrated their Ball Game players. The Maya built huge ball courts, many hectares big, to accommodate the matches. These were built in the city's sacred precinct, suggesting that the game had a sacred, ritual meaning to it. One ancient dig at Monte Albán, Oaxaca reveals an I-shaped court that was typical for the game. The ruins at Epiclassic El Tajín (650 – 900 CE) show a 60m long ball court, thought to be the typical size of a ball court. Some cities had several ball courts—the city of El Tajín had at least 11.

But, unlike football today, the stakes for Maya were much higher. One of their mythological tales is of their god Hun Hunahpús who later became the Maize god. He was tricked into descending into the Underworld where he was challenged to a Ball Game and lost to the Lords of Death (another tale we'll explore in Part 2). They chopped his head off as punishment. Echoing this tale, the Maya Ball Game was often a matter of life and death. Some archaeologists also believe that the game was used for divination purposes to foretell the future.

The rules of the game were quite simple—the players, all male and working in teams of two or three—had to get a solid rubber ball through a ring high up on a wall. But they were not allowed to use their hands when playing, hitting the ball with their padded elbows, knees, thighs, and shoulders. The game was certainly not for the fainthearted, as the rubber ball could be a lethal weapon. Weighing anywhere from 0.5 to 3.5kg and measuring somewhere between 10 and 30cm in diameter, the ball could easily injure a player and break their bones. That's why warriors and war captives were often forced to play the game. Since the game had a religious significance, the captain of the losing team or sometimes *the entire team* were sacrificed to the gods.

But if you happened to be among the lucky few who won the game, you'd earn yourself huge admiration from the crowd and a special trophy—a *hacha* (a representation of or an actual human head) or a *palma* (a trophy or an element of ceremonial costume). Your fame might spread to the nearby villages, and you'd be invited to compete in some inter-city matches. Maybe it was all worth it in the end.

Chapter 5: The Decline of the Maya Civilization and Human Sacrifice

By the time the Postclassic period arrived, most of the great Maya stone cities were abandoned. And yet a few remained and continued to flourish from AD 900 to 1500. These included the city-states of Chichen Itza, Uxmal, and Mayapán.

Maya cities had always been apart, as opposed to another well-known Mesoamerican tribe, the Aztecs. In other words, there was no such thing as a "Maya kingdom." Because their power wasn't centralized, as in the case of the Aztecs, may be why the Maya survived much longer than the Aztecs. But the Maya did share one important feature with the Aztecs—human sacrifice.

The extent of human sacrifice that was carried out daily in Mesoamerica shocked even the fierce Spanish conquistadors. Bernal Díaz del Castillo, a Spanish soldier who served under Hernán Cortés, recorded some spectacularly gruesome tales in his diary *The True History of the Conquest of New Spain* that he wrote as a memoir late in his life. We'll look at human sacrifice and some of his tales in more detail, to get the full picture of the lifestyle that these ancient cultures led. But first, let's take a look at what life was like for Maya in Mesoamerica in the Postclassic period.

Early Postclassic – AD 1000 to 1250

As we already established, for reasons as yet unknown, the Maya civilization went into decline in the late Classic period. Although we don't know what caused this move, we do know that people abandoned their homes to move to other city-states, where circumstances were more favorable. Thus, the once spectacular cities in the southern lowlands were abandoned. As the Maya moved to the region of Yucatan to make a new start, the northern cities of the region began to thrive.

The city of Chichen Itza dominated the region throughout the Early Postclassic period, up until AD 1250. To understand how the Maya lived in those days, let's take a look at the city and some of its main features.

Inside Chichen Itza – features of Maya cities

The great city of Chichen Itza was such an important economical and political center for the Maya that many historians believe it was even honored in later Mesoamerican literature, referred to as one of the great mythical cities or *Tollans*. The city became a regional capital around AD 600. It continued to thrive until its decline in AD 1000.

The name Chichen Itza translates into something like "at the mouth of the well of Itza." "Chi" stands for "mouth" or "edge" and ch'en stands for "well." Itza were a group that gained dominance in the northern peninsula, and their name stands for "enchanter of the water." Thus, the full name would read as "at the mouth of the well of the water enchanter." Isn't it fabulous how much meaning Maya could convey using just a few words?

Excavations of the ruins of this ancient city reveal a marvellous mix of architectural styles. This is why many archaeologists believe that Chichen Itza had the most diverse mix of population among all of the ancient Maya cities. And it's remained popular ever since—1.4 million tourists visit this area every year. So what attracts these tourists to visit, and what attracted the migrating Maya in the first place?

An important feature of the city is its proximity to one of nature's most important resources—water. There are plenty of rivers in the Yucatan region, many of them extending underground. There are also two large, natural sink holes. These are called "ccnotes," and they provide fresh water supply to the city all year round. Maya who settled in Chichen Itza sacrificed gold, jade, incense, and other artifacts, as well as the notorious human sacrifice, in one of the cenotes known as "Cenote Sagrado" or the "Sacred Cenote."

Chichen Itza was extremely well-planned. There are four clusters within the city, containing a great variety of notable buildings. Among other structures, these include the Great Ball Court, Temple of the Jaguars, Thousand Column Market, Venus Platform, Ossario pyramid, the Akab Dzib temple, and El Caracol (the Maya Observatory). Not to mention the city's most spectacular construction, the one that remains favored by the city's many tourists today—the majestic Kukulkan pyramid.

The Maya were seasoned astronomers. They knew a lot about the stars—probably more than most of us do today, were it not for our advanced telescopes and satellite stations. For Maya, among other things, watching the stars was a way to measure time. That's why many of the buildings inside Chichen Itza and other Maya cities reflect major astrological events. Let's explore some of the most impressive buildings in Chichen Itza to better understand how the Maya lived in this period.

The Maya Observatory (El Caracol)

Many of Maya astrological practices continue to puzzle archaeologists to this day. It is difficult to imagine how this ancient civilization predicted the movements of the planets with such precision, without the advanced telescopes and equipment that is available to us today. For example, El Caracol on the site of Chichen Itza is believed to be linked to the orbit of Venus. The front staircase of this building targets the most northern position of Venus. And during the summer solstice sunrise and the winter solstice sunset, the corners of this building align with the position of the sun. That's some engineering, isn't it?

The Great Ball Court

We already learned about the ancient Maya Ball Game in the previous chapter and its significance among the Mesoamerican cultures. Chichen Itza was no different—it had several ball courts, including its most impressive one, the Great Ball Court. It was so impressive in fact that it did not have a rival in all of ancient Mesoamerica, measuring 166 x 68 metres lengthwise, with two huge 12m tall walls.

The Kukulkan pyramid

Also known as El Castillo, this ancient temple has been built in perfect harmony with the Maya Solar Calendar in the number of its steps, its geometry, and design. To this day, the March Spring Equinox remains the most popular day to visit Chichen Itza, attracting thousands of spectators. They watch in awe as the sun hits the nine main terraces of the Kukulkan pyramid, causing a serpent-like shadow to slither along its northern staircase. That's where the pyramid gets its name from—translated from Maya, it's called "Feathered Serpent." It's amazing to watch this event— just as the Maya did thousands of years ago!

Human sacrifice

Let's now tackle one of the most dreaded but also fascinating features of Maya civilization— human sacrifice. From the perspective of our culture, where acts of violence are punished, it may be tempting to overlook the aspect of human sacrifice and its significance for the ancient Maya. We may be drawn to focus on the more enlightened aspects, such as the spectacular Maya art, architecture, and cosmology. But dismissing or minimizing the importance of human sacrifice for the Maya civilization would mean missing the full picture of how this ancient society functioned. So let's explore the tradition of human sacrifice in Chichen Itza and its wider significance for the Maya civilization.

Human sacrifice was practiced by Maya throughout the ages. Apparently only introduced after the Toltec era, the earliest evidence found dates back to the Classic period (starting with AD 250) and it carried on until the 17th century, right through to the very last stages of the Spanish conquest. But why did Maya, otherwise advanced and seemingly enlightened, engage in these gruesome rituals? To understand this, we must first understand the way the ancient Maya thought.

Life for Maya was unpredictable and largely down to the whims of nature. If there was enough rainfall and the right amount of sunshine, their crops would yield a good harvest. If there wasn't, then their population would suffer. It's easy to see how a culture that felt powerful and safe behind the stone walls of its great cities could have felt completely helpless at the same time, when it came to predicting the patterns of nature. What's more, the Maya did not have the scientific view that most of us possess these days. We see cause and effect in nature, we understand how our actions could be impacting our environment, but science has shed a light on these issues. Because we can understand them better, most of us don't feel the need to make sacrifices to any deities. It was not so for the Maya. Although many things in their civilization were indeed advanced, including their understanding of the medicinal plants and healing practices, they lived in an age where everything that happened to them was closely linked to the spiritual realm. Although they treated illnesses with the use of their plants, they saw the act of healing as an interaction between the spirit of a certain plant and the spirit of the person who was sick. Just as nature was whimsical and unpredictable, so were the moods of their gods. They needed to be pleased in order to avoid the next catastrophe. This is where human sacrifice came in. It was an essential part of everyday existence, and people were not only sacrificed to the gods, they also performed acts of self-mutilation. What's more, many of them did so willingly.

The Maya saw blood as sacred, a potent source of nourishment for their deities. To sacrifice a living creature meant offering the highest prize available to the gods. Human life was the ultimate offering, the culmination of many annual ceremonies and rituals.

The methods of human sacrifice

Warning—this part of the chapter is not for the squeamish, so only read on if you feel you can handle it! It's a natural reaction for most of us to turn away from acts of violence, or to be disgusted by them. For the Maya, however, ritual sacrifice took many forms and often constituted a part of a public celebration. Decapitation, the removal of a still-beating heart and bow-and-arrow sacrifice were among the most popular methods. The sacrifice of a foreign king was seen as a particularly potent offering.

Archaeologists working at Chichen Itza have found decapitation depicted on reliefs in two of the city's ball courts, including the Great Ball Court. As we explored in earlier chapters, it wasn't uncommon for the losing captain or the entire team to be sacrificed after an important ballgame match. The inhabitants of Chichen Itza used other methods, too. During times of drought, famine, or disease humans were hurled into the Sacred Cenote, a sinkhole that was 50m wide with a drop of 20m. All this to appease the many gods and deities that we'll explore in a later chapter.

Although Maya society was becoming more and more secular all the way through the Postclassic period, human sacrifice carried on well after the decline of Chichen Itza, after the Spanish had conquered Yucatan—the same region where they first encountered the Maya.

Chapter 6: Late Postclassic Period and the Spanish Conquest

AD 1250 marks the start of the Late Postclassic period. It lasted until the Spanish invasion in AD 1521. Of course, Maya continued to exist long after this date, and we'll look at what modern Maya get up to today in the next chapter. But for now, let's take a look at what happened to the Maya in the Late Postclassic period.

Before the arrival of the conquistadors

We already learned how important Chichen Itza was in the Postclassic period, along with other great cities in Yucatan, including Mayapan and Izamal. Far from being friendly, these cities actually rivaled each other.

There is an ancient legend surrounding Chac Xib Chac, the leader of Chichen Itza, and Hunac Ceel, the ruler of Mayapan. The latter convinced Chac Xib Chac to steal the bride of the ruler of Izamal (a story that echoes something we may be more familiar with in the West—the events leading up to the Trojan war that was allegedly sparked with the kidnap of Helen of Sparta who later became the princess of Troy).

Naturally, the rulers of Izamal responded with violence and defeated Chichen Itza, driving its inhabitants from their city. Hunac Ceel's plan to weaken his neighboring cities had succeeded.

But where did the surviving Itza go from there? Many left Yucatan and moved south, founding a new island capital named Tah Itza. With the population of Izta gone, the stage was set for the Mayapan to take the spotlight, their ruling family Cocom becoming the most powerful lineage in the entire region.

The Cocoms were power-hungry. They demanded all the leaders of the surrounding allied provinces to come and live at Mayapan. This became the "league of Mayapan," with 16 allied city-states. But it didn't last long. In AD 1444, the Xiu lineage rose up against the Cocoms, succeeding in defeating them. The league became disbanded. The 16 city-states that were allies before became rivals once again, enmeshed in civil wars until the day the Spanish set foot on their shores.

The arrival of the Spanish

We've mentioned the Spanish a lot, but why did they come all that long way to South America in the first place? To answer that question, we must travel back in time, all the way back to AD 1504 in Medellin, Spain. This is when a university dropout named Hernando Cortés, aged only 19 at the time, set sail to Santo Domingo (modern Dominican Republic). Motivated by tales of adventure and the great fortune that was rumored to be abundant in the recently discovered Mexico, he embarked on an expedition in AD 1518. He was accompanied by Bernal Díaz del Castillo who later became the governor of Guatemala and wrote an account of his travels with Cortés in his memoir *The True History of the Conquest of New Spain.*

His memoirs paint a picture of adventure and danger, and gruesome human sacrifice that they encountered on their way to the exotic Aztec city of Tenochtitlan. His memoirs also give an insight into the personality and motivations of Cortés. He's portrayed as a man of valor and courage, one who tried negotiating with the locals before attacking them. He left an icon of the Catholic St Mary, Mother of Jesus at the sight of each conquest, trying to convert the locals to their new religion. But, like many of his contemporaries, Cortés seemed to have been motivated more by his thirst for silver, gold, and power than his mission to spread the Catholic faith.

Yucatan is where the Spanish first encountered the Maya. According to Díaz, their first contact with the locals was rather unsuccessful.

"They led us to some very large buildings of fine masonry which were the prayerhouses of their idols, the walls of which were painted with the figures of great serpents and evil-looking gods. In the middle was something like an altar, covered with clotted blood, and on the other side of the idols were symbols like crosses, and all were coloured. We stood astonished, never having seen or heard of such things before."

This early encounter culminated with the battle at Champoton, where the Spanish barely escaped with their lives. The conquest of New Spain was certainly no walk in the park.

But the conquistadors were determined. Armed by their thirst for the treasures that were rumored to be in Mesoamerica, they pressed on. They'd brought with them glass beads that the locals gladly accepted in exchange for various goods. For them, gold and silver was not valuable at all, and many of them used cocoa beans as currency. Here's what you could get with cocoa beans back in the day.

Just four cocoa beans could buy you an entire pumpkin, one of the staple foods in Mesoamerica. If you had 10 beans, you could either buy an entire rabbit or ask a lady to spend the night with you. This is another proof of cultural variation—what one person sees as valuable, another dismisses as trash.

The conquest of New Spain

Cortés wasn't all that interested in the Maya. In fact, his mind was set on the Aztec kingdom of Tenochtitlán. Many archaeologists believe that the Spanish arrival in the great Aztec city coincided with their prophecy of the arrival of a white-skinned god. Because of this, Montezuma welcomed Cortés' expedition with open arms, showering the Spaniards in lavish gifts. But it wasn't long before a revolt broke out and Cortés captured Montezuma. Several battles later, Cortés was finally able to establish a new city on the ruins of Tenochtitlán that he called Mexico City. He ruled with an iron fist, inflicting cruel punishments on the indigenous people of Mesoamerica. Many more were killed by the diseases that the Europeans introduced, such as smallpox.

So much for the Aztecs. But what happened to the Maya? As we already discussed, the Maya kingdom was not united at the time. In fact, it was split into 16 rival city-states or provinces. This was actually beneficial to the Maya. While the Aztecs had one centralised seat of power in their great city of Tenochtitlán, the Maya were not as easy to capture. Their rivalries with the Aztecs often led them to aid the Spanish in their conquest. The Maya Itza kingdom in the southern part of Yucatan was hostile to its neighbors during this time of military alarm. Thanks to this, the Maya were able to maintain their independence for nearly two more centuries. It was only in AD 1696 that the Spanish finally captured the last of the Maya city-states, the Itza of Tayasal.

But what happened to the Maya after their last cities were invaded by the Spanish? Well, there are still plenty of Maya around. Most of them live in modern Belize and the Peten of Guatemala, proudly tracing their ancestry back to the times of ancient civilization when the Maya were a powerful force to be reckoned with. Next, let's look at how the modern Maya live today, including the rituals that they still observe.

Chapter 7: Maya Today

The Maya are indeed well and alive today, with many of their sacred rituals becoming entwined with more modern practices. As is often the case when different cultures clash, the Spanish conquest created a great deal of overlap between the Mesoamerican and European religions, namely the Maya worldview and the Christian belief system. There were many similarities, such as the burning of incense during religious rituals, the worship of images, the hierarchy of priests, a ritual calendar, and pilgrimages based around it.

As well as inhabiting the aforementioned areas of Belize and Guatemala, populations of indigenous Maya can also be found in the western parts of Honduras and El Salvador and some Mexican states, including Yucatan, Campeche, Quintana Roo, Tabasco, and Chiapas.

In fact, there are roughly six million Maya still around today, and their lineage is evident in their family names, their looks, and their language, distinct from any other in the surrounding area. What's more, some Maya have even gone on to receive international acclaim.

Meet Rigoberta Menchú Tum, a political activist from Guatemala. She's set on defending the rights of the indigenous people in Guatemala, especially women. In 1992, she received the Nobel Peace Prize. She also ran for president of Guatemala in 2007 and 2011. This is what she says of the Maya people who are still alive today:

"We are not myths of the past, ruins in the jungle or zoos. We are people and we want to be respected, not to be victims of intolerance and racism."

Of course, the Maya have changed since the fall of their great cities in the Postclassic period. But they have managed to preserve many of their ancient traditions, thanks to their extraordinary efforts to maintain their distinct way of life, despite oppression and assimilation attempts. Many of their traditions have changed form, though. Let's examine these, starting with the Maya religion.

Maya religious rites today

While the Maya still observe some of their ancient rites and rituals, their modern belief system is a blend of Catholicism. It's true that their ancient gods have been replaced with statues of saints, but the stories surrounding these saints are far removed from their European roots. Led by both secular and religious rulers, the Maya communities conduct their worship at special shrines set in mountains and caves. They sacrifice candles, incense, and chickens to the saints, accompanied with a ritual alcoholic drink.

Shamans remain important to this day, performing divination, rituals, and keeping a count of the 260-day Maya ritual calendar. In fact, these ancient calendars remain in use by many Maya tribes to this day. The Maya farmers in Yucatan conduct rituals and ceremonies, following the 365-day Haab calendar cycle, especially during Wayeb, the short month of the year that consists of only five days.

You can even find printed Tzolk'in calendars in some areas of Yucatan, while many people in the highlands of Guatemala use the Chol Q'ij printed calendar.

If you want to put yourself in the shocs of modern Maya, try this calendar converter and see for yourself what today would look like in modern time. You can access it at www.maya.nmai.si.edu/calendar/maya-calendar-converter

The role of the calendar keeper

Some Maya villages have specially assigned calendar keepers. The calendar keeper is called Ajq'ij in the Mayan language. They are the people who work "within the living Maya calendar." But not only that. The calendar keepers help support the community in which they live, offering advice to those who need help and by building a support structure for the people. An important role of these spiritual guides is to give thanks for their life and the life of humanity at specially designated altars.

How do the Maya live?

While there are some special roles within the Maya community, reserved for religious and secular leaders, such as the calendar keepers, most Maya are still farmers, just like they have been for thousands of years. They also dress in a distinctive way. The women wear loose hand-woven or embroidered huipiles or blouses. These blouses have a special pattern and color, identifying which community they belong to. The traditional wear for Maya men is a *traje* but many choose not to wear it, as in the highlands of Guatemala it can be dangerous to call attention to themselves as the indigenous people of Maya.

The Maya caught up in military conflict

Unfortunately, many Maya do encounter racism and violence for being different. In the 1980s certain Maya tribes living in Guatemala were caught up in a conflict between guerillas and the government. The guerillas who hid in the forests all around demanded that the Maya provide them with food and shelter. As a result, 150,000 Maya were killed by the Guatemalan death squads, and a further 40,000 disappeared without trace. Thousands of refugees also fled to parts of Mexico and the United States, disrupting their way of life.

The Maya living in Mexico in Chiapas are still caught up in a military conflict—this time between the Zapatista rebels and the government of Mexico. The harvesting of the mahogany trees is also threatening the Maya environment and their unique way of life.

Maya medicine

The Maya healing practices are an important part of their way of life. The ancient Maya civilizations had a wealth of knowledge surrounding the medicinal qualities of certain plants. Still wary of foreign invaders who might steal or destroy their knowledge, many indigenous tribes still possess this medicinal knowledge and keep it well hidden from curious eyes and ears. Many of their healing practices are based on this ancient knowledge, showing astonishing results. While we cannot tap into all their secrets, here are three concepts that we *can* learn from the ancient Maya that can help us live well today.

1. Eat foods that are good for you—eating avocado, chia seeds, corn, sweet potatoes, pumpkins, beans, tomatoes, and lean meats can help boost your immune system, if consumed as part of a healthy and balanced diet. Chia seeds in particular contain substances that help prevent cancer and provide the body with much-needed omega-3 fatty acids. Let's not forget cacao that Maya consumed daily—it's packed with antioxidants and is high in certain minerals, such as magnesium, calcium, iron, copper, zinc, and potassium. Take care to avoid cacao drinks that are packed with sugars though—the Maya called their hot chocolate drink "bitter water" for good reason!

2. The body and soul are part of the same thing. Thanks to religious indoctrination that was rampant throughout the centuries, many of us have inherited a subconscious belief that the soul is somehow superior to the body. But the Maya saw good health as a sign of a well-balanced life. The Maya used a mixture of healing herbs and potions, massage, hydrotherapy, and prayer to heal various ailments in a holistic way. This, the Maya

believed, would balance the flow of ch'ulel, a sort of life-force energy that they believed flowed through each person.

3. Live your life according to the natural cycles in nature. Since the invention of electricity, we've come to believe that we can function well at almost any time of day. But nature still exerts powerful influence over us, and some events that happen in our lives are simply out of our control. While we all want to be happy, suffering is often unavoidable. The Maya saw life as a continuum—a series of birth and death cycles. Termination followed regeneration, and seeing this wider meaning of life events may have helped the Maya to live with lowered stress levels and more feelings of serenity.

It seems that the ancient wisdom of the Maya is still relevant today. Take some of these beads of wisdom and weave them into the fabric of your daily life to find better health, peace, and serenity.

Part 2 – Mythology

Chapter 8: Maya Creation Story

One of the riches that the Maya civilization has left behind is their wonderful mythology. As professor Edwin Barnhart explains in his audio-lecture series, it's important to understand that for a Maya, mythology was woven into their daily lives. In other words, there was no separation between their myths and their reality. Everything that happened to them in life could be explained by events occurring in the spirit realm. So it was with their story of the creation of the world. For the Maya, this was more than a beautiful story—it was evident in their daily life.

Not only was the creation story passed down orally from generation to generation, it was also emulated in their art and ceramics. Earlier this year, the Los Angeles County Museum of Art (LACMA) in the USA hosted a fascinating exhibition titled *Revealing Creation: The Science and Art of Ancient Maya Ceramics.* The exhibition did exactly what it says, "on the tin"—it offered new insight into the ancient Maya civilization, combining evidence gained from technical analysis of Maya ceramic vessels with the information that is known about the Maya. The exhibition considered ancient Maya ceramic production as both art and science, emulating acts of primordial creation.

The Popol Vuh

Around 1704, a Dominican priest by the name of Francísco Ximénez gained the trust of the local Maya at Santo Tomás Chichicastennago where he served. After the slaughter and the diseases that the European settlers had brought upon the Maya, it could not have been an easy task!

But Father Ximénez was determined. Armed with his knowledge of the indigenous Mesoamerican language Cakchiquel and his charm, he gained the approval of the Maya who lived in the area. He was allowed to behold something that no other European was allowed to see—the Maya creation story, known as the Popol Vuh or "The Book of The Community." At some point in the Maya history, their creation story was written down, and this is what Father Ximénez was allowed to see. He transcribed and translated the Popol Vuh, making it accessible to the Europeans, and allowing curious explorers to learn of the marvels of Maya mythology to this day.

In the beginning

The Maya creation story was developed from the particular environment that these people inhabited. That's why the creation story is so tied in with their calendar system, as well as the establishment of the rain and corn cycles. Now, let's delve deeper into this wonderful story.

In the beginning there was only stillness. No light, no Earth, no living creatures—only endless sea and silence. Six deities lay in these waters, and decided to create Earth. These were Framer and Shaper, Tepew and Quetzal Serpent, Xpiyacóc and Xmucané. They helped Hurakán (or "Heart of Sky") to accomplish the task.

Framer and Shaper (both male and female) modeled the Earth, using their words only, echoing other ancient creation stories. The gods then planted a ceiba tree, to separate the sky from the Earth and make space for all life. The roots of this magical tree reached deep down into the Maya Underworld, penetrating its nine levels. However, its branches reached up, touching all thirteen levels of the Maya Heavens.

The gods wanted to create beings that could keep time and worship them. I think you'll agree that it's not an easy task! Indeed, it even took the gods several attempts to get it right. After creating plants, the gods then created animals. But naturally they could not speak to or worship them.

So they set about creating human beings from mud. But these beings had no soul. They were stiff, and they couldn't procreate. The gods sent a great flood upon the "mud people" and destroyed them.

The gods tried again. This time, they shaped people from wood, which they thought to be a better material. While the "wood people" were strong, their minds and hearts were not properly formed. And they were cruel towards animals. So, as a punishment, the gods ordered the animals to eat the "wood people," and so they did. Those lucky few who survived hid high up in the trees, and are said to have become monkeys. By the way, the evidence of the sad fate of the "wood people" can still be found on certain Maya pottery pieces.

The Maya Hero Twins

The story of the Hero Twins outlined in the Popol Vuh is deeply entwined with Maya cosmology. You see, the Maya saw all events in terms of their spiritual causes. That's why worship to appease spiritual deities was so important to them. And so their calendar, based on their observations of the Earth and the planets, was shaped with a view that a certain deity looked after each aspect of the calendar. But let's get back to our creation story ...

After the "wood people" had been destroyed, the creation of Earth was almost complete. There was Sky and Earth, plants and animals, but no human beings to roam the Earth. And no Sun or Moon existed as of yet. Then, a vain bird by the name of Seven Macaw decided to claim that he was the Sun and the Moon, thanks to his shining feathers and jewelled eyes.

The Maya Hero Twins, Hunajpu and Xbalanqué, were annoyed by the bird's arrogance. And so they defeated Seven Macaw—they shot him with darts from their blow-guns. It wasn't just the bird that they defeated. They took on the Lords of Death who dwelled in the Underworld.

The Maya Hero Twins were keen Ball Game players, just like their father who'd been killed by the Lords of Death. These lords were annoyed by the loud noises that the twins made while playing the Ball Game, so they ordered the twins to play against them in Xibalbá in the Underworld. They had played a similar trick on their father Hun Hunahpu, shaming him with several impossible trials before they decapitated him.

After the Maya Hero Twins survived the trials with cunning trickery of their own and defeated the Lords of Death, they resurrected their father. He came back to life as one of the most important deities in Maya religion, the Maize god.

But what became of the Maya Hero Twins themselves? Remember the arrogant bird who claimed to be the Sun and the Moon? Well, at this point in the creation story, the Earth still had no Sun or Moon to shine over it. So the Maya Hero Twins became heroes once again. They climbed up to the sky and became the Sun and the Moon, illuminating the Earth.

The creation of man

Now that the Sun and Moon shone over the Earth, the gods could make one final attempt at creating human beings. Finally their efforts paid off—and perhaps more than they'd anticipated ...

The gods mixed yellow and white corn with water, and this became human flesh. This is what the Popol Vuh says about the first four men (echoing the four cardinal directions of the Maya cosmology) of this creation who walked the Earth:

"This time the beings shaped by the gods are everything they hoped for and more: not only do the first four men pray to their makers, but they have perfect vision and therefore perfect knowledge."

Their perfection alarmed the gods—they had simply wanted to create beings who could keep time and worship them. But instead, they'd created beings who could become like gods themselves. This time, instead of destroying them, the gods put a fog upon the people's eyes so they could not perceive their own divinity. Then they created wives for the first men, and these couples then created the leading Quiché lineage as they reproduced.

Chapter 9: The Maya Cosmology

We already looked at the Maya calendar and their creation story, but now let's look at their cosmology.

The Maya believed that their day of creation was August 11, 3114 BC. They believed in recurring cycles of creation and destruction lasting about 5,200 years. According to the Maya Long Count calendar, that cycle finished in AD 2012, marking a new era in the story of human civilization.

Now, in order to understand and appreciate their cosmology, you must put yourself in the shoes of a typical Maya. Forget all you learnt about gravity, the laws of physics, and the spherical nature of our planet. Here are some basic beliefs that you would have held about the world and the Universe, if you were an average Maya living some thousands of years ago.

- **The Earth is flat and four-cornered.** Each corner had its own color—East was red, North was white, West was black, and South was yellow. There was also a central point that was green. What's more, each corner was located at a cardinal point.
- **The Sky was held up by magical beings.** Some Maya believed that the Sky was supported at four corners by four gods who possessed incredible strength. They called them *Bacabs*. Others believed that the Sky was supported by four trees. The green *ceiba* tree that was mentioned in the creation story stood at the center of the Earth.
- **The Earth was actually the back of a giant crocodile.** Yep, that's right. And the crocodile was resting idly in a pool of water lilies. It had a buddy or a counterpart in the sky, a double-headed serpent. It's worth noting that the Maya word for "sky" is similar to their word for "snake."
- **Heaven had 13 layers.** Naturally, each layer had its own god. The *muan* screech-owl bird looked after the uppermost layer.
- **The Underworld had nine layers.** Each corresponded to one of their Lords of the Night. It was a cold and unhappy place. Sadly, most Maya believed that this is where they'd end up after they died. They would enter the Underworld through a cave or a cenote, like the Sacred Cenote in Chichen Itza. Of course, you had a better fate if you were a king—you'd

still end up in the Underworld but because of your supernatural powers you'd be reborn in the Sky World and become a god.

- **There were many, many, *many gods*.** At least 166 named deities had been found, but there may have been more. Each god had many aspects—some were transgendered, others could be both young and old. This is known as the Maya pantheon.

- **There was one supreme God.** That was Itzamná, responsible for introducing writing, arts, and sciences. Echoing many other ancient myths, his wife was Ix Chel, the goddess of the Moon. She also looked after the craft of weaving, as well as medicine and childbirth.

So those are the basic principles of what would have formed your world-view, had you been born a Maya in the ancient world. Now, let's look at some of the rituals you would have followed and the role of the priests that you would have honored.

As we already discussed, religious rites and rituals were important among the Maya. This meant that besides the king, the most important person you could ever encounter was the priest.

The role of the priests

Unlike many modern-day priests, the ancient Maya priests were allowed to marry and procreate, often passing their knowledge and rights to their sons. Their role was closely connected to the Maya calendar and their view of astronomy.

But being a priest was no walk in the park. The ancient Maya priests had many responsibilities. They calculated time, induced festivals and ceremonies, set fateful days and seasons, performed divination, cured diseases, conducted writing and genealogies. You could say that the Maya clergy were in charge of religion, the spiritual well-being of their people, and the preservation of their history.

The Maya rituals were dictated by the 260-day Sacred Round calendar. The religious rites and performances all had a symbolic meaning. People observed strict rules surrounding these events, such as sexual abstinence and self-mutilation. We already looked at the role of human sacrifice in the Maya world, but it's important to note that many people were proud to perform acts of self-mutilation. Ritual bloodletting was seen at every important calendar event or festivity, performed by kings and commoners alike. It was considered as a way to send human energy skyward and receive divine power in return. When the Maya civilization began to fall, rulers who moved from one city to the next performed many bloodletting rituals to maintain their power.

During ritual dancing and dramas, kings and noble people often entered a visionary trance, where they were transformed into gods. The king was thus a vessel for bringing supernatural powers and prophecies down to Earth, and relating these to his people for the benefit of all. Shamans were also often present during human sacrifice and divination ceremonies.

A very important study that informed the Maya rites, rituals, and ceremonies, as well as their world-view, was astronomy.

Astronomy and the ancient Maya

It's amazing how accurate the Maya and their Mesoamerican counterparts were when it came to calculating their calendar, in accordance to their knowledge of astronomy. The Maya cycles, calculated in 260-day and 365-day periods, are a perfect match to the actual solar year in the tropics. The margin of error is only 19 minutes! And all this without modern telescopes or scientific equipment.

Their calendar is largely based on the observations of the movements of the Sun, recorded in detail by their priest-astronomers. Using a forked stick, these priests had only their naked eye and the recorded knowledge of their forefathers available as tools to calculate the path of Venus and other celestial bodies.

Nonetheless, they were able to predict events, such as the solar eclipse, with incredible precision. As we already discussed, the architecture of their great pyramids was aligned with the movements of the Sun during the spring and autumn equinoxes. They did this to venerate the gods. Let's look at one spectacular example, called the Temple of the Inscriptions at Palenque that houses the tomb of one of Maya civilization's great rulers—Pacal.

Pacal's tomb and the descent of the Sun

Unlike most Maya rulers and kings, Pacal was not born of kings. His mother and great-grandmother, two powerful women of their era, were said to have ruled as true kings. Thanks to their reputation, Pacal was able to defy the laws and stereotypes of his time and become a king himself. To support his claims, he argued that his mother was the First Mother who created both gods and humans, descended upon Earth as a living creature. Pacal also claimed that his date of birth was the same as that of the great goddess, and therefore he was the son of the goddess. It seemed to have convinced the priests, and that was just as well, as the people of Palenque were better for it.

During his and his son Chan-Bahlum's reign, art and architecture flourished in Palenque. Naturally, people wanted to commemorate him, and so when he died around AD 650, at the grand old age of 80, the people of Palenque built him an astounding sarcophagus. Its lid alone weighed five tons! That's almost the same as four compact cars put together. The sarcophagus weighed more than 15 tons. Naturally, such a sarcophagus could not be buried just anywhere. And so the construction of the great Temple of the Inscriptions began.

The structure of this temple, like the many impressive buildings for the ancient Maya, aligned with the Sun. During winter solstice, the Sun sets behind the high ridge beyond the temple, and lines up with the center of the temple roof. When the Sun crosses the sky, its rays shine through the doorway inside the temple. They hit the back wall of the temple and, as the Sun descends, its rays seem to travel down into Pacal's tomb. It symbolizes the Sun's death. Its entry into the Underworld is a match for the same journey for Pacal.

The importance of astronomy and rituals

Not only architecture was ordered around the movements of celestial bodies for the Maya, symbols of celestial bodies and rituals around the planetary movements were also present. For example, many of the Maya murals and carvings show deities of the heavens. These include a sort of a sky-band, made up of various symbols woven together in a chain. These represented the Moon, the Sun, the planet Venus, as well as night, day, and the sky itself. Not only did the Maya believe that their rulers would go to Heavens after they died—they also believed that they had a mandate in heaven. Thus, many were represented carrying decorated sky-bands in their hands.

While the celestial bodies did possess supernatural powers and special ritual importance, the Maya also believed that the Sun and the Moon needed their help. When they set, these celestial bodies journeyed through the Underworld, constantly threatened by the Lords of Darkness, just like the Maya Hero Twins had been. How could Maya help them? By sacrificing, of course.

To fully understand and appreciate the Maya mind-set, far removed from our own, you need to understand that many Maya performed ritual sacrifice willingly, and thought to gain immortality, if they offered themselves up in order to continue the cycles of the Universe.

The planet Venus

As you may have noticed, the planet Venus is particularly important for the Maya. Their god Quetzalcoatl is identified with Venus. One of the very few surviving written Maya chronicles, the Dresden Codex, contains predictions, tables, prophecies, and other important elements that track the movements of Venus. This planet was an important omen for the Maya. It provided guidance for ritual activity and prompted important battles. The Dresden Codex was also an important correction tool for the skilled Maya astronomers.

Conclusion

The history of the Maya is a tale of vivid characters, ingenuity, and, above all, endurance. The Maya have survived and thrived for many thousands of years, and continue to preserve and observe their native customs even to this day.

In this book, we've aimed to summarize the most important and interesting events in the Maya history, from the beginnings of this ancient culture in the Archaic period many thousands of years ago, through to modern day and the surviving Maya villages in South America. By doing so, we hope to have provided you with an insight into this fascinating culture—not only in the chronological events that took place in their history, but also the way these ancient people lived their daily lives, the gods they worshipped, and the customs they observed. From hunter-gatherers to farmers, Ball Game players, priests and kings, the Maya and their customs continue to astonish us to this day.

The Maya history would not be complete without their mythology and cosmology accounts. Some of their religious practices may have left you feeling a bit queasy, especially when we talked about the more gruesome rituals involving human sacrifice. But all history needs to be understood in its cultural context, and the ancient Maya were certainly different from us and even their descendants who are alive today.

It may not be possible to fully grasp the splendor and norms that were commonplace for the Maya, so we hope that this book has provided you with enough insight to embark on your own journey of discovery. We hope that the endnotes, the maps, and the images of important settlements that we have provided in the next section will guide you on your way!

Endnotes

Introduction:

1. Rovirosa-Madrazo, C. (2017). *The Maya are alive – and have made some wise recent predictions | Citlali Rovirosa-Madrazo.* [online] the Guardian. Available at: https://www.theguardian.com/commentisfree/2012/dec/21/maya-zapatistas-predictions [Accessed 5 Aug. 2017].
2. Web.stanford.edu. (2017). *The Maya Civilization – Present and Past.* [online] Available at: https://web.stanford.edu/class/e297c/trade_environment/photo/hmayan.html [Accessed 3 Aug. 2017].

Part 1

Chapter 1:

1. Historymuseum.ca. (2017). *Civilization.ca – Mystery of the Maya – The Maya today.* [online] Available at: http://www.historymuseum.ca/cmc/exhibitions/civil/maya/mmc08eng.shtml [Accessed 4 Aug. 2017].
2. Rath, T. (2017). *Archaic Period – National Institute of Culture and History.* [online] Nichbelize.org. Available at: http://www.nichbelize.org/ia-archaeology/archaic-period.html [Accessed 3 Aug. 2017].
3. News.nationalgeographic.com. (2017). *New Evidence Unearthed for the Origins of the Maya.* [online] Available at: http://news.nationalgeographic.com/news/2013/13/130425-maya-origins-olmec-pyramid-ceibal-inomata-archaeology-science/ [Accessed 5 Aug. 2017].
4. Mark, J. (2017). *Maya Civilization.* [online] Ancient History Encyclopedia. Available at: http://www.ancient.eu/Maya_Civilization/ [Accessed 4 Aug. 2017].

Chapter 2:

1. Houston, Stephen D. *Function and Meaning in Classic Maya Architecture.* Washington, D.C.: Dumbarton Oaks Research Library and Collection, 1998. Print.

2. Marcus, J. (1992). Review: Cuello: An Early Maya Community in Belize by Norman Hammond. *Journal of Field Archaeology*, 19 (3), 397-399. DOI: 10.2307/529926. Retrieved from URL [http://www.jstor.org/stable/529926]

3. Chiapadecorzo.byu.edu. (2017). *Chiapa de Corzo Archaeological Project*. [online] Available at: http://chiapadecorzo.byu.edu/ [Accessed 3 Aug. 2017].

4. National Geographic. (2017). *Maya Calendars Actually Predict That Life Goes On.* [online] News.nationalgeographic.com. Available at: http://news.nationalgeographic.com/news/2012/12/121207-maya-truly-did-not-predict-doomsday-apocalypse/ [Accessed 2 Aug. 2017].

5. BBC News. (2017). *'Oldest Maya tomb' found in Guatemala's Retalhuleu* – BBC News. [online] Available at: http://www.bbc.co.uk/news/world-latin-america-20091121 [Accessed 3 Aug. 2017].

Chapter 4:

1. Theinitialjourney.com. (2017). *Maya Beauty | Revelations* – The Initial Journey. [online] Available at: http://www.theinitialjourney.com/life-issues/mayan-beauty/ [Accessed 4 Aug. 2017].

2. Cartwright, M. and Cartwright, M. (2017). *Maya Food & Agriculture*. [online] Ancient History Encyclopedia. Available at: http://www.ancient.eu/article/802/ [Accessed 2 Aug. 2017].

3. Olver, L. (2017). *TheFood Timeline: Aztec, Maya & Inca foods*. [online] Foodtimeline.org. Available at: http://www.foodtimeline.org/foodmaya.html#maya [Accessed 3 Aug. 2017].

4. National Geographic. (2017). *Top 10 Foods of the Maya World* [online] Nationalgeographic.com. Available at: http://www.nationalgeographic.com/travel/top-10/maya-foods/ [Accessed 2 Aug. 2017].

Chapter 5:

1. Haciendachichen.com. (2017). *Chichen Itza facts – Yucatan, Mexico – Chichen Itza architecture, Maya pyramids, Cenotes, Hotels*. Chichen Itza's wildlife: flora and fauna. Places to visit in Chichen Itza, Yucatan, Mexico. [online] Available at: http://www.haciendachichen.com/Chichen Itza-Yucatan.htm [Accessed 5 Aug. 2017].

2. Díaz, B. *The Conquest of New Spain*. UK: Penguin, 2003. Print.

Chapter 6:

1. Rath, T. (2017). *Late Postclassic – National Institute of Culture and History*. [online] Nichbelize.org. Available at: http://www.nichbelize.org/ia-archaeology/late-postclassic.html [Accessed 2 Aug. 2017].
2. Perry, Richard D. *Exploring Yucatan: A Traveler's Anthology*. Santa Barbara: Espadana Press, 2001. Google books. Web. [Accessed 5 Aug. 2017].

Chapter 7

1. Ngm.nationalgeographic.com. (2017). *National Geographic Magazine – NGM.com*. [online] Available at: http://ngm.nationalgeographic.com/geopedia/Maya [Accessed 3 Aug. 2017].
2. Criscenzo.com. (2017). *The Maya Today*. [online] Available at: http://www.criscenzo.com/jaguarsun/mayanow.html [Accessed 5 Aug. 2017].
3. YouTube. (2017). *The work of K'iche' Day Keepers*. [online] Available at: https://www.youtube.com/watch?v=ZGQZ3xLqOoQ [Accessed 4 Aug. 2017].
4. HuffPost. (2017). *What The Ancient Maya Can Teach Us About Living Well*. [online] Available at: http://www.huffingtonpost.com/2014/01/03/ancient-mayan-health_n_4482382.html [Accessed 6 Aug. 2017].

Part 2

Chapter 8:

1. Barnhart, E. (2015). *Maya to Aztec: Ancient Mesoamerica Revealed*. The Great Courses. [Audiobook].
2. Lacma.org. (2017). *Revealing Creation: The Science and Art of Ancient Maya Ceramics* [online] Available at: http://www.lacma.org/art/exhibition/revealing-creation [Accessed 3 Aug. 2017].
3. Bassie, K. (2012). *Maya Creator Gods*. [online] Mesoweb. Available www.mesoweb.com/features/bassie/CreatorGods/CreatorGods.pdf [Accessed 3 Aug. 2017].

Chapter 9:

1. Historymuseum.ca. (2017). *Civilization.ca – Mystery of the Maya – Astronomy*. [online] Available at

http://www.historymuseum.ca/cmc/exhibitions/civil/maya/mmc07eng.shtml#cycles [Accessed 3 Aug. 2017].

2. Historymuseum.ca. (2017). *Civilization.ca – Mystery of the Maya – Cosmology and religion*. [online] Available at:

3. http://www.historymuseum.ca/cmc/exhibitions/civil/maya/mmc03eng.shtml [Accessed 4 Aug. 2017].

4. National Geographic. (2017). *Have We Been Misreading a Crucial Maya Codex for Centuries?* [online] News.nationalgeographic.com. Available at: http://news.nationalgeographic.com/2016/08/maya-calendar-dresden-codex-venus-tables-archaeology-science/ [Accessed 3 Aug. 2017].

5. Ancient Origins. (2017). *The Maya myth of creation*. [online] Available at: http://www.ancient-origins.net/human-origins-folklore/maya-myth-creation-0063 [Accessed 5 Aug. 2017].

Appendix 1:

Maps of important settlements

Maya capital cities

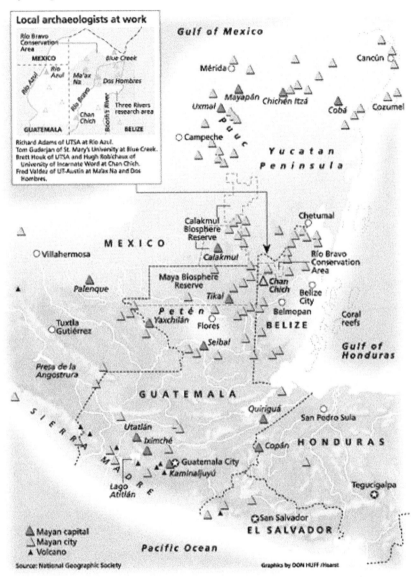

Available from http://www.globalsherpa.org/wp-content/uploads/2011/03/mayan-capitals-cities-map.jpg

The Maya ruins at Lamanai, Belize

Available from http://globalsherpa.org/mayan-civilization-ruins-sites-culture-calendar-2012/

The Maya ruins at Tikal in Guatemala

Available from http://globalsherpa.org/mayan-civilization-ruins-sites-culture-calendar-2012/

A map of Chicehn Itza

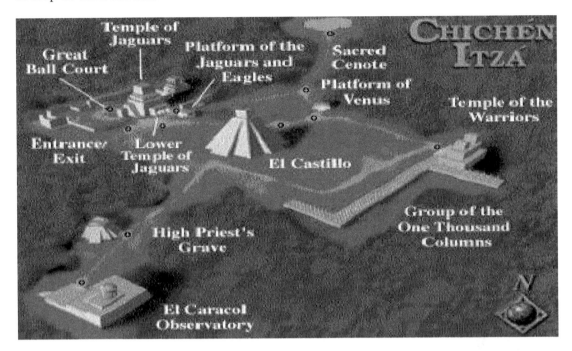

Available from http://www.haciendachichen.com/Chichen Itza-Yucatan.htm

The Kukulkan pyramid at Chichen Itza

Available from http://www.expeterra.com/Expeterra%20Chichen%20Itza.html

The Maya calendar

Available at http://www.crystalinks.com/mayancalendar.html

The Dresden Codex

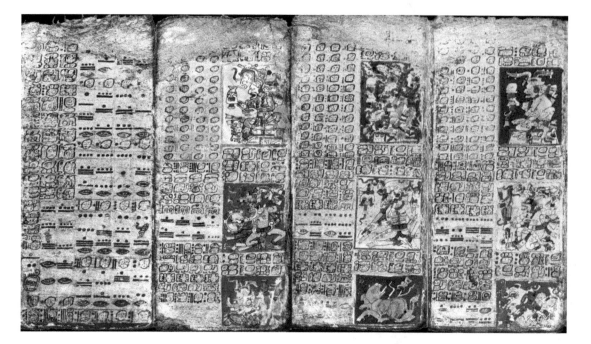

Available at http://www.latinamericanstudies.org/dresden-codex.htm

Maya people today

Available at http://www.kidzworld.com/article/26424-all-about-mayan-culture

Can you help?

If you enjoyed this particular part on Mayan Civilization, then it would be really appreciated it if you would post a short review for the book on Amazon.

Thanks for your support!

Part 2: Aztec

A Captivating Guide to Aztec History and the Triple Alliance of Tenochtitlan, Tetzcoco, and Tlacopan

Introduction

Nothing remains of the ancient Mesoamerican civilization who called themselves the Mexica, better known to us as the Aztecs. Nothing except for their remarkable story.

In this book, we discuss their enigmatic origins and how the Aztecs rose from nomadic tribes to the dominant power in Mesoamerica at an astounding speed. You'll wander the streets of their great capital city of Tenochtitlán, known as "the Venice of the New World" among the Spanish Conquistadors, who spread the term all over Europe. You'll discover the full extent of the city's splendour, visiting its many market stalls, smelling fresh chocolate and vanilla pods. You'll indulge in a taste of ripe, hand-picked avocados and freshly baked corn tortillas, as you decipher Náhuatl, the language spoken by the 50,000 merchants who visited Tenochtitlán every day.

You'll probably wonder how this great city, built in the middle of a lake and isolated by two of Mexico's highest mountains, Iztaccihuatl and Popocatepetl, could ever be defeated. From the arrival of the first Spaniards in 1519 to the eventual fall of the Aztec empire, we'll talk you through the major battles that eventually led to its fall. We'll uncover lies and deceptions in the alliance with their neighbouring cities of Tetzcoco and Tlacopan. We'll also look at Aztec legacy on the world today: how Tenochtitlán became the basis for the capital of the New World and evolved into today's Mexico City.

Remember the most interesting stories are peppered with fascinating contrasts and paradoxes. Perhaps this is what makes the Aztecs so interesting. They emulated and idolized the Toltec civilization in everything they did, although there's no archeological evidence to support that the great Toltec civilization even existed. Each year, the Aztecs performed a substantial number of brutal human sacrifices, yet they were also completely devoted to intellectual pursuits, such as mathematics, public speaking, and the arts.

Masters of their own fate, the Aztecs re-wrote their story of origin, burning their history books. This has enmeshed much of their history with mythology and made it difficult to separate myth from fact. Further complications were caused by the Spanish conquistadors and their successors, who wanted to portray themselves in a good light or justify their conquest when writing their accounts of the Aztecs.

Chapter 1 – The Origins of Aztecs: A Tribe Destined for Greatness

On the Mexican flag backdrop of a vertical tricolour of green, white, and red, a fierce eagle sits on top of a cactus plant, wrestling with a snake that it's snatched in its mouth. This is the symbol of the Aztec city of Tenochtitlán and tells the story of how a humble tribe from the North, who called themselves the Mexica, rose to astonishing wealth and power just a few hundred years after finding their 'promised land,' known today as Mexico City.

Let's look at the origins of the Mexica civilization, better known to us by the name of the Aztecs.

Rewriting Aztec history

The story of their origin is obscured by legend. The Aztecs arrived and settled in the Valley of Mexico around the year 1250 AD, and they most likely came from the North. Thanks to a tyrannical move by one of their kings, Itzcoatl, who ruled the Aztec empire from 1427 to 1440, all the books that told the story of Aztec history up to that point were burned.

The son of a slave woman and a nobleman, Itzcoatl quickly rose to power, thanks to his military achievements. He was set for greatness, and, perhaps to erase his heritage of being born to a slave woman, he made earnest efforts to rewrite the history of the Aztecs to create a more palatable version of their origins.

Another book-burning incident took place much later, destroying more crucial information about the Aztecs. It was done to heavily censor the Florentine Codex, a 12-volume work by the Franciscan monk Bernardino de Sahagún. He spent years interviewing the local tribes, learning about the ancient Aztec language of Náhuatl and their many rites and customs. When he returned to Europe in 1585, the Spanish authorities confiscated much of his original material, destroying this valuable resource. The later versions of the Florentine Codex that did get published were most likely heavily censored, erasing many captivating details that would have shed light on the Aztecs and other ancient Mesoamerican cultures.

Because of these unfortunate instances, what we know of the origins of the Aztec civilization are draped in myth, and subject to much speculation by archaeologists and historians.

Aztlán - the cradle of Aztec civilization

Aztlán is a bit like Atlantis, a legendary ancient land that disappeared and has puzzled researchers for years. Even the Aztecs were fascinated with finding the mystical land of Aztlán. Similar to King Arthur's mission to find the Holy Grail, the Aztec ruler Montezuma I gathered his fiercest warriors and most knowledgeable scholars in the 1450s and sent them on a mission to find Aztlán. Apparently, they succeeded, although the maps they drew have not survived, so their success remains debatable. It was said to be located somewhere to the north of Tenochtitlán, and, like the Aztecs' great city, Aztlán too was in the middle of a lake.

While it could be nothing more than Aztec propaganda to depict an idealized version of their origins and to support their claim of rulership, the myth of Aztlán is fascinating. It was incredibly important to the Aztecs too - the term Aztec means "the people of Aztlán." Although the Aztecs called themselves the Mexica, they did regard themselves as the direct descendants of the tribe that used to live in Aztlán.

The myth of Aztlán

When the Spanish arrived in Mexico in the 16th century, they became fascinated by the Aztec culture. They made several attempts to document their origin story, and parts of it were recorded by Diego Duran, a Dominican friar who arrived in the New World in 1540 when he was five years old. A document called *Los Anales de Tlatelolco* (The Annals of Tlatelolco), now held at the National Library of France in Paris, also reveals much about the lost land of Aztlán.

These accounts reveal the fascinating story of Aztlán and the origins of the Aztec civilization. Translated, the word "Aztlán" stands for "the place of white birds" or "the place of herons." According to legend, the Aztec emerged from the hollow earth through a system of caves, along with six other tribes (Acolhua, Chalca, Tepaneca, Tlahuica, Tlaxcalan, and Xochimilca).

A depiction of Chicomoztoc — the place of the seven caves. Source: https://en.wikipedia.org/wiki/Aztl%C3%A1n

The seven tribes wandered the Earth together, sometime between the years of 1100 and 1300. Then the other tribes decided to migrate south while the Aztecs remained in the north. They eventually found their "paradise," called Aztlán. It was a large island in the middle of lake Metztliapan ("the lake of the Moon").

The science of linguistics can help trace the true origins of Aztlán. The Aztec language of Náhuatl comes from the Uto-Aztecan language tree. Robert Bitto explores this further in his podcast

Journey to Aztlán, the Mythical Homeland of the Aztecs. He explains that several tribes who lived to the north of Mexico spoke a language that belonged to the same language tree. Along with some indigenous tribes from northern Mexico, these include the Hopi, the Pima, and the Utes of Utah, USA. The linguistic connection stretches as far as Idaho and Montana, supporting the claim the Aztecs did come from the north. Scholars agree the most likely location for Aztlán is in the northern or central parts of Mexico.

Considering that Aztlán was as good as paradise, why did the Aztecs decide to leave?

The fall of Aztlán

Some accounts state the Aztecs fled because they were encroached upon by a tyrannical ruling elite that wanted them expelled or enslaved. Once they began to flee, they were pushed further and further south by the Chichimecas, a warlike marauding tribe.

Other accounts state there was a natural disaster of such a magnitude it drove the Aztecs out of the area and forced them to migrate south. Climatic studies conducted in the region support this claim, stating that between the years of 1100 and 1300 a mass migration occurred to the south-west of the modern-day United States. This was most likely because of a lengthy period of drought. The Aztecs left the area around 1200 AD, so this theory is plausible.

After leaving Aztlán, the Aztecs became a nomadic tribe, wandering the plains of northern Mexico, and making their way south for two hundred years. They endured many hardships along the way before they eventually settled on the tiny island in the middle of Lake Texcoco in the Valley of Mexico, where they founded their great city of Tenochtitlán. According to legend, the Aztecs were guided and seen through their hardships by a deity called Huitzilopochtli, the Aztec god of war, the sun, and human sacrifice. He was later the patron god of the city of Tenochtitlán.

But it wasn't a straight journey, and by no means easy either. The Aztecs made several stops along the way, even settling temporarily in some of these areas. At times, some of the Aztecs wanted to remain and began opposing the priests who urged them to keep moving. Battles broke out amidst their own people, as they wandered the land for nearly two hundred years, from hardship to hardship. Until they finally arrived in the Valley of Mexico. But the welcome they received wasn't quite what they'd expected.

Chapter 2 – The Unwelcome Arrival in Mexico Valley

After two hundred years of exile, the Aztec was on a quest to find a new homeland. They had finally reached the Valley of Mexico, where their priests had guided them and instructed them to settle. However, they were not welcomed by the locals, who were wary of foreigners. Their journey had been hard, but life was not about to get any easier for the Aztecs.

They arrived in the Valley of Mexico around the year 1300 AD. The valley was bustling with various tribes and civilizations, most of them rivals. Professor Edwin Barnhart explains what happened to the Aztecs after they arrived in Mexico Valley and before they founded their great capital of Tenochtitlán in chapter 33 of his lecture series *Maya to Aztec: Ancient Mesoamerica Revealed*. According to him, the Aztecs were "outnumbered, outranked, and outclassed," a stark contrast to the bustling civilization the Spaniards found just over 200 years later.

Two of these rival tribes were larger than the rest - the Tepanecs and the Culhuacan. The Tepanecs allowed the Aztecs to settle, granting them Chapultepec or "the grasshopper hill." It was situated on the west shore of Lake Texcoco, now the central park of Mexico City. Their subway system also features icons relating back to this period - one of the stops is depicted as a hill with an ant on it, symbolizing the grasshopper hill.

The Tepanecs were a dominant force in the area, taking over after the Toltec empire fell around 1200 AD. Many cultures around the time, including the Aztecs, went to great lengths to claim themselves as descendants of the ancient Toltec civilization and to emulate their achievements. However, the Toltec civilization may have never existed at all.

Settling in Chapultepec

It wasn't long before the Teponecs grew annoyed with the Aztecs. Less than a year later, they kicked them out. At this point in history, the Aztecs acted like savages. They didn't pay their tributes to the Tepanecs, and were considered uncultured savages.

The Aztecs fled Chapultepec and travelled south. They reached the area controlled by the Culhuacan, who granted the Aztecs a barren land known as Tizapan. It was infertile and impossible to farm. The Aztec diet consisted mainly of lizards and rodents.

But their god Huitzilipochtli was never far from them, at least according to the Aztec priests who provided guidance. They said the Aztecs should take up deeds that honoured the war god and do the 'dirty work' that no one else wanted to do. This helped the Aztecs to develop a sophisticated warrior culture.

This tactic paid off. Twenty years later, the Aztecs had intermarried with the people of Culhuacan and their children were immersed in their culture. After more than two hundred years of unrest, things were finally looking up for the Aztecs, until one fatal day that changed everything.

Sacrifice gone wrong

It's important to understand the meaning of human sacrifice for the Aztecs. They believed sacrifice was a welcome offering to their gods, and many people gladly engaged in acts of self-mutilation. Sacrifice was often a way to get closer to the gods, so when Achicometl, the ruler of Culhuacan, offered his daughter to the Aztecs for marriage in 1323, they thought it would be a better idea to sacrifice her to their gods. In turn, this would make the king's daughter into a goddess.

Except Achicometl did not see it that way. One day, he saw one of the Aztec priests wearing the flayed skin of his daughter during a festival dinner. Far from thanking the Aztecs for their attempt to make his daughter into a deity, he was so horrified he cast them out. Somewhat confused, the Aztecs were forced to wander the Valley of Mexico once more.

The vision of their new home

One day, as they wandered around Lake Texcoco to find their new home, their high priest had a vision. "Our promised land will be marked by an eagle, sat on a cactus, holding a snake in its mouth," he announced, coming out of his trance. The Aztecs didn't have their own land yet, but at least they had a sign of what they were looking for.

The symbol of an eagle sat on a cactus with a snake in its mouth on the flag of Mexico. Source: https://www.tripsavvy.com/the-mexican-flag-1588860

Hopeful, they settled with the Teponecs once again. Having learned their lesson, the Aztecs paid tribute to the Teponecs and fought for them. They added more problems in the valley where several tribes and cultures were already fighting each other. They fought against Culhuacan while searching for the sacred sign that would mark their new home.

Two years later, their priest finally saw the sign. Huitzilipochtli certainly wasn't giving them an easy time - their promised land was in the middle of a lake on a tiny island. Shallow, marshy land made up the island, but the Aztecs followed their god and settled there. In 1325, the Aztecs began to build Tenochtitlán on the island. Little did they know that a hundred years later the Aztecs would dominate the entire region, and this tiny island would become one of the greatest cities that Mesoamerica had ever seen.

Building a city on a lake

The land that the Aztecs found was just a tiny island, surrounded by a lake. They employed a local farming method called *chinampa*. They created artificial islands in the lake by piling up mud and soil in the shallow lake bed. These islands looked like small, rectangular areas where the Aztecs could grow crops. According to Jorge, M et al., these measured at 30 m × 2.5 m and the Aztecs measured these beds in *matl* (one *matl* was equivalent to 1.67 m). First, they marked the limits of the soil bed by using stakes they pushed into the shallow lake bed. Next, they fenced it off in a rectangle, using a lightweight construction material called wattle. They made it by weaving thin branches together and tying them to upright stakes to form a woven lattice.

This was demanding work, but it paid off because the soil was incredibly fertile for planting crops. Although they were still paying tribute to the Tepanecs, in time, they could live on their land autonomously and grow crops. What's more, the area was defensible because it was perched in the middle of a lake and surrounded by water.

Life was still tough for the Aztecs. Jose Luis de Rojas, an anthropologist from the University of Madrid, wrote that "early years were difficult." People lived in huts, and even the temples dedicated to Huitzilopochtli were made of "perishable material." But day-by-day, their territory expanded until in 1325 they named their new city Tenochtitlán.

Chapter 3 – The Rise of Tenochtitlán and the Triple Alliance

"To give an account … of the greatness, and the strange and marvelous things of this great city of Tenochtitlán … and of all the dominions and splendor of Moctezuma its sovereign; of all the rites and customs which these people practice, and of the order prevailing in the government, not only of this city but also of others belonging to this lord, much time and many very expert narrators would be required."

This is what Hernando Cortés wrote to Holy Roman Emperor Charles V in 1520 regarding what he saw in the great Aztec city of Tenochtitlán. It was a city built entirely on a lake, with canal transport systems, rivalled only by the Italian city of Venice. Beautiful temples adorned the streets of this great city, among them the Aztecs' greatest gem - the principal temple that, according to Cortés, could easily house an entire town of 500 inhabitants.

This was only 200 years after the Aztecs founded their great city. So how did Tenochtitlán rise from an uninhabited tiny island in the middle of a lake to the greatest and most splendid fortress that Mesoamerica had ever seen?

Let's visit 1325 again. The Aztecs paid tribute to the Tepanecs during this period. They helped the Tepanecs to conquer more land, achieving greater riches. As their wealth increased, so did the wealth of the Aztecs. But they were still not entirely free. However, in 1427 the Aztec leader Itzcoatl decided to take some bold and drastic steps to take control back. He forged a powerful alliance with two other city-states, Tetzcoco and Tlacopan, also known as the Triple Alliance. Together, they conquered the Tepanec rulers and their great wealth transferred to the Aztecs and their allies.

The Triple Alliance

When the three tribes (the Aztecs, Acolhua, and Tepanec) came together to create a triple alliance of their respective cities, it created a powerful military force. Eventually, the Aztecs used their cunning ways to sack their allies and become the dominant force in the entire region. Who knows how far their empire would have expanded, had it not been for the arrival of the Spanish conquistadors in the year 1519.

The Foundation of the Triple Alliance

Around 1350 AD, the region where the Aztecs dwelled was divided into small, centralized city-states, each with its own ruler and administrative centre. The city-states owned a surrounding area of smaller villages and hamlets that depended upon the city. Some of these cities fought each other, while others had friendlier relationships. They traded with each other and worshipped similar deities. Nonetheless, each wanted to be more powerful than the other.

After much bickering and trading, two city-states became the leaders of the region. These were Tlacopan, ruled by the Tepanecs, and Tetzcoco, home of the Acoulha tribe. At this point, the Aztecs were still paying taxes to the Tepanecs. But all that changed when another city-state, Azcapotzalco, entered the region in 1418.

As the power of Azcapotzalco increased, the Aztecs were forced to pay more tributes to them. Yet in the year 1428, the Aztecs joined their forces with Tetzcoco and finally revolted against their oppressors. This two-city alliance was gaining some important victories, and after they had proved their worth, the Tepanec city of Tlacopan decided it would be beneficial to join the alliance. This was the birth of the Triple Alliance, and together the three city-states defeated Azcapotzalco.

Confident in their achievements, the three city-states soon realised they could go much further. In 1473, they conquered the entire basin and ruled with an overwhelming military force.

Unequal Rights Within the Alliance

However, despite their quick success, the power within the Triple Alliance was not always equally distributed. Although each city still enjoyed complete political autonomy, the distribution of wealth and the spoils of war was unequal. Usually, an equal amount of the loot went to Tetzcoco and Tenochtitlán (each received ⅖ of the entire amount of goods) while only ⅕ went to Tlacopan, as this city was the last to join the alliance.

Over time, the cities became unequal in other aspects, too. Tenochtitlán later became the military leader, having the strongest army, while Tetzcoco lead in other spheres of life, such as law, engineering, and the arts, which the Aztecs greatly revered and held in high esteem.

Having different strengths allowed the cities to remain the dominant presence in the region, ruling together with their military force, political strategies, and their excellent, ever-expanding trade networks. The Triple Alliance was strengthened further with elite marriages between the noble families. The Triple Alliance grew economically too, as their client states had to pay them taxes in the form of products that freely entered the markets of the three city-states, ensuring a constant supply of trade.

How the Triple Alliance Disintegrated

Since Tenochtitlán was the military leader of the Alliance, its rulers soon realised they could make the final decisions on all military actions. The Aztec rulers began to disintegrate their allied states - first Tlacopan, then Tetzcoco. They were less successful with the latter, and the city-state of Tetzcoco remained independent right up until the arrival of the Spanish. Although Tenochtitlán dominated the alliance, it continued to exist through political, social, and economic means, sharing the common goal of regional domination.

Tenochtitlán's arrogance eventually led to its downfall. Since Tetzcoco had grown hostile towards the alliance and the Aztecs, it later aided Hernando Cortés to overthrow this great city, succeeding in 1591.

Chapter 4 – The Greatest Aztec Kings and Their Heritage

Before we go on to examine all the wonders of the great Aztec city of Tenochtitlán as it would have stood when the Spanish conquistadors found it, let's first get an overview of the greatest Aztec rulers and their accomplishments.

It's important to mention another civilization that the Aztecs tried to emulate in everything they did.

The Toltec heritage

The Aztecs attempted to change their reputation of being savage foreigners. They tried to emulate the Toltec civilization, seen by many Mesoamerican cultures as one of the greatest civilizations that ever existed. Many tried to link their lineage to the Toltecs, who were seen as the supreme example of political leadership, artistic skill, and noble excellency. They were seen a bit like the legendary Atlantis is seen by the modern world - a splendid civilization destroyed by a terrible catastrophe, the origins of which still puzzle many archaeologists and historians to this day. But similar to Atlantis, not much evidence has been found of the existence of a Toltec civilization. Despite the Toltec cult that many Mesoamerican cultures displayed, could it have been nothing more than a myth?

The Aztecs adored the Toltecs - they were the supreme example of leadership and excellency that the Aztecs wanted to aspire to. They believed the Toltecs "taught the clay to lie" with their great artistic abilities. And it wasn't just the Aztecs. The Zapotecs, the Mayan civilization, and pretty much everyone across Mesoamerica loved the Toltecs, holding their civilization in the highest esteem.

The Aztec elite was among the most fervent emulators of the Toltecs. One of the greatest Toltec arts was the art of public speaking. In Náhuatl, the language that the Aztecs spoke, a king was called "Tlatoani" or "the one who speaks."

They also used the Toltec symbolism of eagles and jaguars frequently - it became a signature symbol for the Aztec art of war. Additionally, they built ball courts and skull racks and some very peculiar sacrificial statues, similar to those that the Toltecs had.

Is there any truth in the Toltec myth?

Despite this influence, there is little archaeological evidence found to support the myth of a Toltec civilization. There was a Toltec nation, but their capital city of Tula could hardly be seen called the greatest cradle of Mesoamerican civilization. The city housed approximately 30,000 people during its peak between 900 and 1200 AD. It was surrounded by thousands of stone houses with flat roofs where extended families lived, all crammed together. They did have some workshops inside those houses, but they were simple and small - Tula never reached the great level of artistry that the Aztecs described. Similar to other Mesoamerican nations, the people at Tula had corn in every meal, and they had just enough food to feed their population.

Many archaeologists agree the Toltec empire has been massively overestimated. The Aztecs took steps to recast their own history, so their idealization of the Toltecs may have been spurred on by their propaganda at the time.

Now that we know exactly where the Aztecs had come from and whom they aspired to be let's take a quick look at their greatest kings and their most notable achievements.

Acamapichtli, The First Aztec Ruler (1375 - 1395)

Acamapichtli's name translates as "a handful of reeds." He was the first leader of the Aztecs (note that they did not have an empire yet). Originally from Tetzcoco, Acamapichtli was only 20 years old when he became the leader of the Aztecs, thanks to his ties with other important families and his bold claims to be a direct descendant of the Toltecs whom the Aztecs idealized.

He arrived in Tenochtitlán and was received with great ceremony. During the 19 years of his reign, Acamapichtli married several times (Aztec rulers could have more than one wife). To strengthen the strategic ties between the city, he married Ilancueitl, the daughter of the ruler of Culhuacán. He also married a wife from each of Tenochtitlán's four *calpullis,* or districts.

He expanded the city's farmland on the lake while trying to hold off the hostile Azcapotzalco forces, to whom Tenochtitlán paid tribute each year. The first Aztec laws emerged during his reign, along with stone houses that replaced houses made of cane and reeds. He was an excellent politician and managed to strengthen his position by remaining diplomatic and clever, rather than forceful.

Acamapichtli is believed to have founded the Great Pyramid or Templo Mayor of Tenochtitlán, an architectural wonder that would not be fully completed until 1487.

The reigns of Huitzilihuitl, Chimalpopoca, and Itzcóatl (1396 - 1440)

A depiction of Huitzilihuitl. Source: https://en.wikipedia.org/wiki/Huitzilihuitl

Huitzilihuitl carried on with the clever trade negotiations started by his father. He married the daughter of the ruler of Azcapotzalco, whom the Aztecs still paid tribute to. His second wife gave birth to Moctezuma I, who would later succeed the throne. Huitzilihuitl built a port and vastly expanded the cotton trade. Later, he aided his father-in-law in his attempts to attack Tetzcoco and succeeded in sacking many important cities around the region. He died around 1417, succeeded by Chimalpopoca.

Chimalpopoca ruled Tenochtitlán for about nine years. The attempts to secure more control over the region by Azcapotzalco's rulers eventually led to Chimalpopoca's assassination and the exile of Tetzcoco's ruler. However, this sparked the idea of the Triple Alliance. Azcapotzalco's aggression led to talks between Itzcóatl, Chimalpopoca's successor, and the rulers of Tetzcoco and Tlacopan who worked together to form the Triple Alliance and defend themselves against Azcapotzalco. In 1428, their efforts succeeded and they conquered Atzcapotzalco.

Moctezuma I - the first ruler of the Aztec Empire (1440 - 1469)

Moctezuma I as depicted in Codex Mendoza. Source: https://en.wikipedia.org/wiki/Moctezuma_I

Moctezuma I was the son of Huitzilihuitl and the first king of Tenochtitlán who really represented the city's wealth, independence, and power. During his uncle Itzcóatl's reign, Moctezuma I became one of his strongest supporters. He is believed to have been a wise ruler and a fierce warrior and statesman. Thanks to his efforts, he created order, in the quickly growing Aztec empire while expanding its borders. His first successful war campaign was against the city of Chalco and was followed by many other victories.

However, Moctezuma had his fair share of troubles. A four-year drought that fell upon the region led to starvation among his people, and many of the Aztecs died. Other natural disasters, such as heavy snow, floods, and frost destroyed the crops. Nonetheless, he created order and restored Tenochtitlán's prosperity through his war efforts, trade links, and diplomatic negotiations.

Moctezuma I was a good leader in war. He was also a brilliant statesman, and he understood the need for advancement not only in his war efforts but in the education of his people. He wanted them to become more sophisticated, and have a stronger sense of an identity - he wanted his people to be proud of who they were and where they came from. He introduced many innovative ideas to his people. He ordered the rewriting of Aztec history and reworked the Aztec calendar. Moctezuma I was the one who organised an expedition to find the mythical land of Aztlán, from which the Mexica were believed to have emerged.

He was also an innovator. Moctezuma I brought a fresh water supply to the city and implemented important laws to keep order within the society. He also ordered the construction of fascinating sculptures, stunning temples, and beautiful botanical gardens.

He introduced a new tradition, called Guerra Florida or "The Wars of Flowers." These were ritual wars, fought between the members of the Triple Alliance and their enemies. The two armies would meet on an established date at an agreed location that would later become a sacred site. This meant a far lesser cost to either party than an actual war. The start of the war was announced by the burning of a pyre of paper and incense in between the two armies, which consisted of an equal number of participants. The use of different weapons was also restricted, and the Aztecs preferred to use weapons that would require a close proximity to their enemies.

Although the "Flower Wars" usually meant that fewer soldiers were needed for the battles, it was usually the nobles who fought in these wars. If they happened to die during such a battle, their death was considered especially precious, referred to as *xochimiquiztli*. According to American historian and anthropologist Ross Hassig, this can be translated as "flowery death," "blissful death," or "fortunate death."

Needless to say, Moctezuma I left behind a legacy that would help future Aztec kings build and expand their empire.

The reign of Axayacatl, Tizoc, and Ahuitzotl (1469 - 1502)

Moctezuma I was succeeded by Axayacatl, Itzcóatl's grandson, who was only 19 at the time. Since being a king was not a hereditary privilege in the Aztec world, Axayacatl was elected by the leaders of the Aztec empire and supported by the leaders of Tenochtitlán's allied city-states, Texcoco and Tacuba.

It must have been hard for Axayacatl to compete with the legacy of Moctezuma I, who had ruled the Aztec Empire for almost 30 years. The only way to excel was to build upon the previous ruler's success. Right before his coronation, Axayacatl led an expedition against the rebellious city of Cotaxtla. He brought back prisoners who were used as human sacrifices to the gods during his coronation ceremony.

During his reign, Axayacatl continued his line of work by expanding the Aztec empire through war efforts, diplomacy and trade, and constructing grand public buildings to make Tenochtitlán the most stupendous city in Mesoamerica. He conquered the cities of Toluca, parts of Malinalco and Matlatzinca, Tuxpan.

These victories culminated in his biggest war effort - subduing the Aztec allied city of Tlatelolco in 1473, despite his sister's marriage to its ruler Moquihuix. From then on, Tlatelolco was not permitted to have its own ruler.

However, under Axayacatl's reign, the Aztecs also suffered their biggest military defeat before the arrival of the Spanish. In 1478, he led a poorly planned war expedition against the Tarascans in Michoacan. The Aztecs were greatly outnumbered and suffered a great defeat, with only 200 men returning to Tenochtitlán, most of whom were wounded.

Axayacatl was only 30 when he died, but, in addition to his military exploits, he also ordered the construction of the final phase of the grand temple dedicated to the god Huitzilopochtli, as well as a temple dedicated to the rain god Tlaloc. He also ordered the Aztec calendar to be carved on a massive stone that allowed the Aztecs to measure the time with great precision.

He was succeeded by Tizoc, who ruled for only five years. From 1481 to 1486, he started some monumental projects, such as the rebuilding of the Great Pyramid of Tenochtitlán. According to the Codex of Mendoza, Tizoc conquered many city-states, among them Tonalimoquetzayan, Toxico, Ecatepec, Cillán, Tecaxic, Tolocan, Yancuitlan, Tlappan, Atezcahuacan, Mazatlán, Xochiyetla, Tamapachco, Ecatliquapechco, and Miquetlan. He died of unknown causes - some speculate that he was poisoned while others claim that he died of a deadly illness.

Tizoc was succeeded by Ahuitzotl, the last *tlatoani* before Moctezuma II took the throne. He is remembered as one of the greatest military leaders of Pre-Columbian Mesoamerica. Shortly after his crowning ceremony, he doubled the size of the Aztec empire, conquering the Zapotec, the Mixtec, and many other Mesoamerican tribes. He also expanded the Great Pyramid and the Templo Mayor.

Among some of his most interesting achievements is the successful introduction of a bird species known as the great-tailed grackle into the Valley of Mexico.

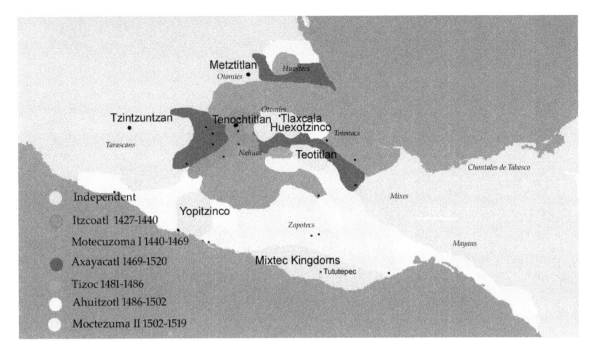

Legend (on map):
- Independent
- Itzcoatl 1427-1440
- Motecuzoma I 1440-1469
- Axayacatl 1469-1520
- Tizoc 1481-1486
- Ahuitzotl 1486-1502
- Moctezuma II 1502-1519

This map shows the expansion of the Aztec empire with each successive ruler. Source:

https://en.wikipedia.org/wiki/Ahuitzotl

Chapter 5 – The Splendor of Tenochtitlán

The ancient Aztec city of Tenochtitlán was truly spectacular. It did not have a rival in all of Mesoamerica, quickly becoming known as the capital of the New World. At the time, Paris only had 150,000 inhabitants, whereas Tenochtitlán housed 200,000 with around 50,000 people attending the bustling market stalls every day.

The construction of Tenochtitlán and its rise to become a successful and bustling city is a testimony to what can be achieved with hard work and ingenuity. By combining the two, it took the Aztecs only two years to turn the tiny island in the middle of Lake Texcoco into the capital of the New World.

Europe could not compete with the sophistication of the city, with its water aqueducts, zoos, and exotic gardens. When the Spanish Conquistadors, led by Hernando Cortés, first set foot on the land of Tenochtitlán in November 1519, it was like nothing they'd ever seen before. Nothing could match either the splendor of the city nor its thirst for human sacrifice.

The Aztec world needs to be viewed through two seemingly opposing lenses. One is their reverence for the arts, poetry, music, and beauty. The other is their love of human sacrifice. Thousands of people were sacrificed in the many temples across Tenochtitlán every year, and this went hand-in-hand with their more palatable religious rites and rituals.

Social order

There were several social castes in the Aztec world, and the higher you were, the more privileges you could enjoy. However, in higher castes, the social norms you had to obey were stricter.

The life of a slave in the Aztec world

Slaves were bought and sold daily in the central market place. They had a designated area, like the other merchants like potters or jewellers. Slaves were at the very bottom of the social order, but they did have some rights. Anyone could end up a slave. If you didn't pay your debts or gambled too much, if you were a foreign captive or if you committed crimes, you might become a slave to pay your dues. Some people sold themselves into slavery to rid themselves of debts or families sometimes sold their children so they could support the rest of the family.

Slave owners had an obligation to feed and house their slaves. The slave's loss of freedom was reported in official documents and decrees.

Your fortune as a slave depended on who purchased you. Because you couldn't decide who that would be, you'd likely pray you were bought by a noble who wanted you to be their servant. Unfortunately for some slaves, priests could also buy slaves specifically for sacrifice. But many noble houses had slaves as servants, and they could live comfortable lives. They could even have time off and earn some money. They could marry and have children, and their children were not considered slaves but free men. Thus slavery was not considered hereditary.

The life of a commoner

This was the biggest social class in the ancient Aztec world, making up about 95% of the population. Most commoners were farmers (who usually tended the land that belonged to the nobles) or craftsmen who did pottery or woodwork, among other trades. Some of them were also soldiers, but all Aztec men were warriors at heart. They had to complete military service for the Aztec army as part of their obligations, and all boys, commoners, and nobles, started learning the art of war from a young age.

As in most ancient societies, fate was very different for women. They were expected to stay at home, doing textiles, cleaning the house, and cooking for the family. They were also the most frequent visitors to the nearby markets.

The families of commoners lived in one-room houses that were made of reed walls and wattle. There were no windows and only one door. They slept on simple reed mats and had a hearth inside that kept them warm during cold nights. Children stayed at home to learn the trade of their parents or they went to school as early as age five (only boys).

They lived like this in tiny districts, where four or five families, usually blood-related, shared the same patio. Each of these areas had a *temazcal* (a type of a sweat bath or lodge that translates as "house of heat"). Children were often born inside the *temazcal*.

Each noble usually ruled over a neighbourhood of commoners who belonged to them. The noble would assign labour in that neighbourhood, and they had a small palace inside the neighbourhood. There would also be a temple and a school for children to attend free of charge, and sometimes even a small ball court for the famous Rubber Ballgame that was popular across Mesoamerica.

The middle class and travelling merchants

The Aztec middle class was made up of travelling merchants. But they were much more than just traders of exotic goods. The merchants served the king himself as diplomats or spies, who assessed if new lands were suitable for conquest while away on their missions, which could last several months at a time. It was a dangerous vocation, and they were all trained warriors who carried weapons on them. They hired professional carriers to come along with them on their missions, who were also trained warriors.

There were relatively few merchants around - only 12 merchant guilds existed in Tenochtitlán - and you could only become a merchant by being born into a merchant family. Thus, commoners could not aspire to become merchants. Despite the great wealth the merchants accumulated following their successful trade missions, they could not actively display that wealth. Often, they dressed in rags upon return, because only nobles could dress in expensive capes and wear jewellery that displayed their social status.

The merchants too had social responsibilities - they were also the judges of the markets where the buying and selling of their goods took place, settling disputes among the visitors and stallholders.

The Nobles

The nobles constituted only 5% of the entire population, and commoners or merchants could not aspire to become a noble. Along with the king, they owned Aztec land, and their children were sent to special schools. Whereas the schools for commoners taught the art of war only, these schools would train children in poetry, public speaking, the calendric system, and many other arts and skills the Aztecs held in high esteem. Children leaving these schools were destined to become government officials, high priests, and captains in the Aztec army.

They lived in spacious palaces with stone walls and cedar beams. Whereas the commoners did not have much in their house at all, these nobles enjoyed finely crafted furniture and ate from beautiful plates, allocating many beautiful rooms to their many servants.

They were expected to be model citizens and illuminate the way for the rest. If they misbehaved in any way and broke the social norms, the punishment was more severe than that reserved for commoners who'd committed the same crime. They also had to be more proactive in their social obligations towards the public, organising public feasts, leading labour teams, as well as leading armies.

The King and High Priest

The king was at the very top of the Aztec social hierarchy. The role of the king was not hereditary - even if an Aztec king was your father, you still had to be elected by a group of nobles to become the next ruler. Thus, your status was always based on your merit or how well you'd appeased the nobles. Although a king had his advisors, he would oversee everything from daily sacrifices, to battle and political strategies, as well as negotiations with foreign kings. The king was the father figure of the nation, as well as their spiritual leader, and thus had to set an excellent example.

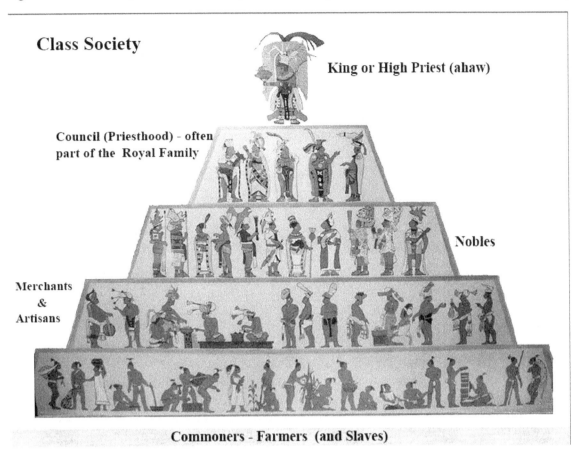

Class Society

King or High Priest (ahaw)

Council (Priesthood) - often part of the Royal Family

Nobles

Merchants & Artisans

Commoners - Farmers (and Slaves)

Aztec social order. Source https://aztecprojectempire.files.wordpress.com/2012/11/social-pyramid.png

Take a walk in the king's shoes

If you were Moctezuma II, you might wake up in your breathtaking and spacious bedroom, possibly next to one of your many beautiful wives.

One of the thousands of servants would help you get dressed. Cleanliness was an important virtue in the Aztec civilization, so you'd wash frequently. After having some breakfast, you'd attend to important stately business. As you wandered through the hundreds of rooms that were reserved for visiting nobles and ambassadors, each with a private en-suite bathroom, on one of the top palace floors, you might catch a glimpse of the priest precinct that was situated right next to the palace, where human sacrifice was part of everyday life. As the head of the state, you'd personally oversee some of them and consult with the high priests to make sure that these rituals were carried out in accordance to the whims of the gods. You probably wouldn't notice how strange it might have appeared to have such beauty and savagery exist right next to each other.

You'd adore the beautiful handcrafted tapestries and murals that adorned the walls, observing good graces by greeting the people you encounter. Hundreds of servants and slaves would emerge from their rooms, ready to attend to your every need. You'd be formal but kind to them, and generous from time to time, as the warm but firm father figure and spiritual leader that you were expected to be.

After you'd walked for what seemed like forever, you'd finally get to the bottom floor, ready for an important meeting. There was never a shortage of them, as being the owner of all the lands in the city and the taxes paid, a lot rested on your shoulders. As well as overseeing the daily sacrifices, you'd be responsible deciding on all the political and battle strategies. Besides, you'd want to keep those nobles who elected you pleased.

You may have to struggle a bit to get through all the gifts piled on the bottom floor from lords and rich visitors who wanted to pay tribute to you and your powerful empire. It wouldn't be unusual if a king from another city had come down to visit you - they had to forge their own political strategies.

Later in the evening, you'd get dressed in your finest clothes, colourfully embroidered and decorated with feathers (the more, the better). You would make your way downstairs for the daily feast, where you'd welcome the new visitor who'd arrived at your palace. You'd want to show off your empire and exhibit good graces to them, so you'd welcome them at your table. It wouldn't be just the two of you though. 300 plates would be on your table alone, all kept warm using a special heating technique, then piled with delicious food from the local market. As soon as you touched any of it, a woman would rush by your side to wash your hands while you enjoyed the festivities and the merriment provided by the many singers, jesters, and dwarfs who were highly esteemed in your country.

Once the feast was finished, you'd leave the room, allowing the hundreds of guards and servants who helped prepare the meal to have their share in the same dining hall. Having cleansed yourself again, you'd go to bed, fast asleep, without the slightest idea that a few centuries later the grand palace you inhabited would lie in ruins, buried under another beautiful building called The National Palace in Mexico City.

Chapter 6 - A Guided Tour Around Tenochtitlán

Let's now take a walk around the rest of the city, parts of which the king would have been able to see through his many, many palace windows.

We have a choice before us - we can travel in a canoe, across the city's many canals (just like people do in Venice). Merchants transported their goods around the city using the canals. Farmers used canoes to get to the lake surrounding the city and to drain the water for planting more crops in the murky waters.

Or we can do something more familiar and simply take a stroll on the ground. Since piloting a canoe might take some training, lct's resort to getting around on our feet, something we're much more familiar with.

Tenochtitlán. Source: https://matadornetwork.com/es/solucion-inundaciones-tenochtitlan/

"Gather for the Official Tour of Tenochtitlán!," you hear a local tour guide shout, waving a feathered pole in his hand. "Come along and discover wonders that you would not encounter even in Europe!"

- Moctezuma II's Palace and his botanical gardens, housing every plant found in Mesoamerica;
- The zoo with the cat-house;
- The aquarium with every exotic fish that lives in the waters near and far;
- The Museum of Ancient Cultures;
- The Public Theatre where people 'dance with their feet;'
- The grand Templo Mayor (or, as you people like to call it, the Great Pyramid of Tenochtitlán).

"And last but by no means least, you'll see with your own eyes the biggest market that anyone has ever seen in all of Mesoamerica, with 50,000 people trading daily! They tell me it's bigger than your modern-day city of London! So, gather and prepare to be amazed!"

In awe, you and the others in your tour group follow the guide as he leads you through the city. It's going to be a long day, filled with adventure and wonder. You'll be gripped by both awe and terror as you unravel the wonders of this city, along with its gruesome tradition of human sacrifice.

The tour begins

You learn the entire city is divided into four major zones called *camps*. Each zone is further divided into twenty districts, commonly known as *calpullis*. Each of these *calpullis* had its own tribe or bloodline living there, with a separate marketplace, temple, and school.

Starting with the least impressive sights to build the tour to a crescendo, your local guide leads you inside one of the city's poorer *calpullis*, where farmers live. You see people emerge from simple huts with thatched roofs, rubbing sleep out of their eyes, wearing little clothing, almost ready to start their day. One of them, a man with coal-dark hair and dark skin that's been scorched in the sun, pops over to tend to his vegetable patch in the garden beside his house. He doesn't even wave hello to you, too preoccupied with the daily grind of his life.

"They can grow food for themselves here," the tour guide explains, after saying something to the man, to which he receives a crabby grunt in reply. You notice that the poor man doesn't have any feathers in the simple garments he's wearing - only nobles could wear feathers, as a sign of class and status.

You're taken aback as a string of children rush out from the same hut, boys and girls ranging from ages of five to fifteen. You wonder how they all fit inside the small hut, but they're all neatly dressed, in poor but clean garments. You ask the tour guide about them.

"They're off to school. Each neighbourhood of the poor has their own market, temple, and school. Girls have a different school to boys, but they all learn the laws and codes of behaviour because they know, even at this early age, that disobeying the law could mean death. That's why it's so important for them to learn this, and to do what society expects of them. Once they reach the age of fifteen, they get separated. The boys go on to learn important skills like hunting, farming, and fighting. The girls stay at home and learn sewing, how to be good mothers and cooks..."

The guide stops half-way, interrupted by a sudden noise. It sounded like a splash, as though something had been thrown in the water. You rush over to the scene, to find people laughing and cheering at a person swimming in the canal. The guide soon joins them.

"It's his birthday today," he explains. "This man was born on the day of air, not a good sign. It means he's destined to be lazy and a drifter. I myself was born on the day of the lizard. It means that I'm destined to become rich. Well, I'm still waiting for that day…"

You learn that this is a typical birthday celebration - friends wake you up by tossing you into a river and later you're obliged to throw them a party where you thank them and everyone who's helped you get to where you are. You ask the guide what would happen to the man if he couldn't afford to throw a feast?

"Well, then he'd be scorned for the rest of the year," he's quick to explain as you leave the scene and carry on with the tour.

Walking along the city's giant causeways

You're excited to see a house where a noble lives - you've heard of how rich and spectacular these could be, and you want to see it with your own eyes. You emerge from the *calpulli* and arrive on one of the three main streets that cross the city, each leading to one of the city's three causeways that connect Tenochtitlán to the mainland of Tepeyac, Ixtapalpa, and Tlacopan.

As you step onto one of the causeways, you're amazed at how accurate one of the Spanish conquistadors, Bernal Díaz was in his autobiographical account, *The Conquest of New Spain*. He said that each causeway was wide enough to fit ten horses, and it really is that huge! They had to be to sustain all the commerce and visitors arriving and leaving the city daily.

"Over there." The guide points in the distance while you wait for one of the draw-bridges to lift and let a boat pass through underneath before you can carry on with your journey. These were also lifted in times of siege when the land needed to be defended, severing mainland access to the city. "Over there is the great Aztec market. It's in the sister city Tlatelolco. The city was established in 1358 and ruled by a Tepanec prince at that time. It became part of Tenochtitlán only in 1473."

In the distance, you can also see lots of tiny islands surrounding the city - they look more like blobs from where you're standing, with ant-like creatures walking around. Those are the farmers, the guide explains, noticing your puzzled gaze. He points to one of the islands. "That's the man we met this morning. He's planting food and flowers using chinampas. We, the Aztec people, are very proud that we can grow everything we need in Tenochtitlán. We can grow our own food and raise our own army. The lake protects us against invaders, and the fertile soil protects our food supply. That's how we started really. We used chinampas, piling mud and muck on top of reed structures, laying low until 1427, when the beautiful part of our city began to emerge. I will show you all of our gems later in the tour."

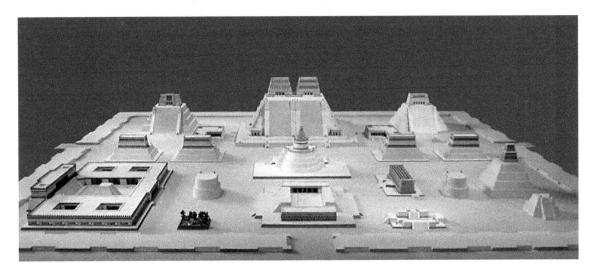

A model of the Templo Mayor precinct. Source http://www.ancient.eu/image/1440/

It's hard to miss the most impressive structure in all Tenochtitlán, as it rises so high it almost clouds the sun. Again, the guide is quick to notice your gaze, and he fills in the blanks in your mind.

"This is our Great Temple or Templo Mayor. In fact, let's go there next, before we visit the nobles' houses, as I'm sure you'll be too preoccupied with its grand structure to focus on anything else."

As you walk the streets, trying to shield yourself from the scorching heat of the sun, you can't help but be amazed at the impressive engineering knowledge that the Aztecs had.

"See all these canals, they actually ensure that the water never grows stale in the lake. It keeps on moving and flowing, so it's always fresh and replenished. One of our great nobles built 16 km worth of walls around the city, to separate the brackish water from the rest of the lake."

He points at a pipe running along the canals and causeways like a giant snake. "Every house has access to tap water - fresh, running water that comes straight from the lake, transported via two massive stone and terracotta pipes via the aqueducts. The pipes go all the way to Chapultepec hill 4 km away. In case you're wondering why we have two pipes, it's to ensure that we always have a working pipe when the other one needs to be cleaned. We Aztecs take great pride in cleanliness, it's a sign of good manners and class."

You ask the guide if you could get a drink of water because the sun is so hot. He says the water in the taps is not potable. He stops at one of the smaller markets on the way and shows you a stall that sells bottled water. You swallow the water thirstily, amazed the ancient Aztecs were drinking bottled water from the nearby springs.

Inside the Temple Mayor precinct

And finally, you've arrived. Templo Mayor is there, right in the middle where all the city's districts meet. You look up, but you can't seem to see the end to its two main towers, accessed by a massive flight of stairs. You know from reading guide books that the pyramid is 60m tall, and stands on a platform of four tiers. Two flights of steps lead up towards its entrance, the western side leading to a summit where two twin temples glisten in the sun, the entire structure painted in bright colours over lime plaster. One is red and the other blue, each representing the colours of a different god.

How tall was Templo Mayor?

The height of Templo Mayor would be equivalent to:

- 14 double-decker buses, stacked on top of each other.
- 8.5 three-story houses.
- a hotel or residential home with 16 stories.

You come back from your daydream, and hear the guide's voice again, loud, and clear, wondering what interesting facts you've missed while you calculated the height of Templo Mayor.

"The Temple is symbolic of Cayutopec: it was built on the very spot where they saw the sign of the cactus, symbolizing the birthplace of their god.

"You're standing at the exact spot where our great god Huitzilopochtli gave his great sign for us, the people of Mexica. This is where our elders saw a cactus with an eagle perched on top, holding a snake in its mouth."

You must wonder if this is what really happened, or if it is just an elaborate fairytale that gave the Aztecs the right to claim the island on the lake.

"We have dedicated our great temple to our war god Huitzilopochtli and our rain god Tlaloc. We thank them for blessing us with a good fortune and keep them appeased by providing regular human sacrifice."

Somewhere in the distance, you feel like you can hear a faint echo of a scream. A woman, a slave or a child perhaps? You came on the tour, mentally prepared for this, but you can't help but shudder.

"Each god has their own requirements," the guide carries on. "Sometimes we need to get children, sometimes foreigners, sometimes people who are willing to be sacrificed, earning themselves honour."

You try to keep calm, suddenly startled by the realisation that although you are a visitor here, you are nonetheless a foreigner.

The guide lines up your group in front of the giant steps and explains more about the temple. "It's taken many lifetimes to build. Our great king Itzcoatl ordered the construction of the temple around 1427 to 1440. Moctezuma I and his successor Ahuitzotl made further improvements, wanting to top their predecessors."

"Today, this temple is what you might call the social and religious centre of our culture. If you stood at the top of the sacred Processional Way during summer equinox, you'd see the sun rising between the two shrines of the upper platform. That's how precise our astronomers and builders were when constructing it."

The guide looks down and instructs you to look around you, while he explains that the entire precinct is 365m wide on each side, surrounded by a wall. "We call it the 'Serpent Wall' because of the snake relief carvings that you can see on the walls."

You take a closer look and run your fingers against the relief on the wall. You are amazed by the detail all along the wall, and as you look around, you try to count how many other buildings are in the precinct, enclosed by its tall walls. You get to 78, when you realise you've drifted off again.

Until now, you've been trying to ignore the wall of skulls at the base of the pyramid, composed of thousands of skulls from sacrificial victims. You're not sure if you want to hear any more detail on this, so you don't ask the guide.

Your attention is suddenly caught by something else - a drunk young man stumbles inside the precinct, pushed along by two heavily armed Aztec guards.

The guide watches him with contempt. "He's a local potter," he says. "Certainly, no noble, but I've seen his stuff being sold at the markets. What a shame that he's given into drinking."

The guards lead him away towards the temple where priests already await them. The man seems so delirious with drink that he does not understand what's going on. Maybe it's for the best.

You tentatively ask the tour guide what will happen to the young man. "He should know better the laws and rules of our society. Lucky for him, he'll be sacrificed to the gods, his body stretched out on a large stone on the top of the pyramid, while a priest slabs an obsidian knife right into his chest and rips his heart out as an offering to the gods."

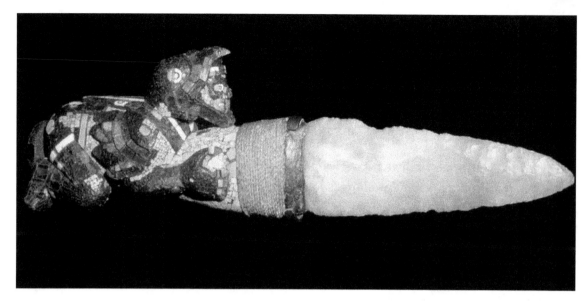

Aztec sacrificial knife. Source: https://www.thoughtco.com/aztec-triple-alliance-170036

The guide tells all this without blinking. Equally calm, he carries on.

"Then he'll be dismembered and decapitated, and what remains of him will be tossed down the steps of the pyramid to land at the base. His fate will be the same as the goddess Coyolxauhqui, who tried to defy our great god Huitzilopochtli."

All this for being drunk, you think to yourself, and decide to watch your alcohol intake at the Aztec feast tonight. You wonder if you should say something, step ahead and defend the young man who simply made a mistake. But you remember how the Aztecs called Hernan Cortes evil, after he criticized their practices, and told him never to say those words again. You remind yourself of the size of the Aztec army and realise that there is nothing you can do, except forget what happened here.

You leave the precinct and Templo Mayor with a knot in your stomach, feeling nauseous. The temple's splendour is overshadowed by what you've learned of Aztec human sacrifices. From reading the guidebooks, you know that thousands of people - somewhere between 10,000 to 80,000, the sources disagree - were sacrificed here on the 7th phase of the temple's inauguration. Either way, the priests had their hands covered in blood for three days. It's hard to imagine that today Mexico City's main plaza stands here.

You wonder how the Spanish conquistadors felt, when they first arrived in the city, amazed by all its wonder and beauty, while disgusted at its brutal practices. But those are the Aztecs; you remind yourself. For all their beauty and love of art, they'll always remain warriors at heart.

Next stop - the zoo!

You're happy to hear that you'll be visiting something more light-hearted next - the city's zoo and its aquarium. From reading, you know that this truly astonished the Spanish conquistadors, who had never seen anything like this before.

First, you're taken to the zoo. By special arrangement, you're granted access to Moctezuma II's castle again, where the zoo is located for his entertainment. You watch many of the 300 zookeepers busy themselves around large and scary animals you've never seen before and, like the Spanish conquistadors, are not able to name, except to say they look like lions.

However, you do recognize some animals that were described by the Franciscan monk Bernardino de Sahagún in the vast, encyclopedic body of work that he created on Aztec customs, rites, and history in the 16th century. Although the church was quick to confiscate much of the material upon his return to Europe, much has survived in a document called the Florentine Codex. Among these are ocelots, bears, some mountain lions, and even eagles. In fact, there's a vast section dedicated specifically to birds of prey, and it looks like the zookeepers are having a hard time keeping them tamed. There's also reptiles, deer, different types of dogs, jaguars, turtles, and rattle-snakes, whom the Spanish conquistadors referred to as "snakes with music in their tails."

It would require an entire day to really appreciate all the animals, and you've got plenty more to see, so the tour guide ushers you on.

Since you're here, the tour guide explains it would be a pity to miss a tour of the botanical gardens also found in Moctezuma II's castle.

The Botanical Gardens

You've already been awestruck by the many gardens you've come across on your walk around the city, by their beauty and arrangements, as well as how well tended they are by the city's many gardeners.

But the Botanical Garden of Tenochtitlán is simply something else. You've never seen such a variety of plants. For the Aztecs, flowers symbolized everything from life to death, from creation to destruction, from friendship to loneliness. Flowers were important, and this was certainly noticeable throughout the botanical garden. In fact, this practice would later inspire botanical gardens all over Europe.

"The botanical garden of Moctezuma II's palace and those established in the king's other residencies are one of a kind," the tour guide explains. "They have hundreds of unique plant species, looked after by specialist gardeners, and if one of the species withers or dies, then an entire expedition is sent out into the lands beyond Tenochtitlán to fetch another sample."

It's certainly impressive, but the aquarium leaves an even bigger impression on you.

The Aquarium and the Museum

A totally novel idea in Europe at the time, ten ponds of salt water and ten ponds of fresh water make up the aquarium. All kinds of fish swim happily around in both. The tour guide leaves the look and structure of these aquariums to your imaginations since not much evidence has remained about them.

You are taken by surprise when the tour guide takes you inside The Museum of Ancient Cultures next. You wander around the building, looking at various artefacts that the Aztecs had collected, many of them believed to be of Toltec and Olmec origin. You're amazed how familiar this feels to visits to your local museums back in the familiar environment of the 21st-century Western world.

The great Aztec jewel - Tlatelolco market

"I hope you are all ready for the final part of the tour. I have saved the best for last, so follow me to the greatest market Mesoamerica and perhaps the entire world has seen until now!"

The tour guide announces, and you set off on your journey to Tlatelolco, the sister city of Tenochtitlan. You encounter street sweepers and gardeners along the way, who seem to be going to great lengths to ensure that the city remains clean and tidy.

At the entrance to the great market, you notice an old man shouting abuse at the people walking past him. Despite his insults, people don't seem to be taking much notice of him. He is clearly drunk, waving a bottle in his hand as he gestures at the other people. Soon, another old man joins him, and together they start dancing around the square like two fools.

Although your first impressions of these men create a strong dislike for them, you can't help but worry about them at the same time. You remember the punishment of the younger man who was drunk, and you worry that the same will happen to the two old men.

"What's going to happen to them?" You ask the tour guide, with doom on your face. You're not sure that you really want to hear the answer.

"What do you mean?" The tour guide looks puzzled.

You voice your concerns about the punishment awaiting them and the tour guide bursts out in hysterical laughter. All eyes are suddenly on you, and suddenly you are afraid of your own fate.

"I've never heard such a thing in my life!" The tour guide says, wiping tears from his eyes. Firstly, he's shocked that you're still thinking about what happened to the young man. Second, he explains that old men in the Aztec world are like gods - they have completed their duties to their elders and raised their children, so they can do whatever they wish and no one bats an eyelid.

You soon forget the incident as the tour guide leads you inside the markets, a sight you'll truly never forget.

Inside the markets

Life is bustling inside the markets, and your eyes dart from stall to stall, from item to item. Everything from pottery to cloth, gold, jewellery, and even slaves are sold.

The tour guide points towards a panel of judges who are settling disputes. To the left of you, a pickpocket is being arrested for trying to steal a jade jewel from one of the stalls. Across from him, a woman has her fortune read while she waits for her husband's hair to be cut.

Opposite you, all kinds of restaurants serve food from all over Mesoamerica. You suddenly notice how hungry you are, so you walk over to one of the stalls to buy some goodies. You sink your teeth inside a freshly baked maize tortilla and a fresh and incredibly ripe roasted avocado. You ask for a cup of Aztec cacao to wash it all down, and it's more bitter and spicy than you had imagined.

While you eat and chat to your fellow tour mates, you watch the Aztec families around you enjoy the performances from dancers, singers, and jugglers balancing logs on their feet as they lay down. You realise the markets are more than just a centre for commerce. For the Aztecs, it's a place for family outings, for catching up on the latest gossip, for taking a break from their duties or work. It is a place to come and be merry. As you stand in the marketplace, watching the various buyers and traders engage with each other, you realise you are standing right in the middle of the beating heart of the Aztec world.

Chapter 7 – Rites, Rituals, and Delicious Recipes

The Aztec calendar relied on a strict set of rules and social restrictions, enforced by law and religious festivities that took place throughout the year, designed to honour the gods, and bring the community together. In this section, you'll learn all about the calendar that directed the execution of some wonderful and some pretty horrific rituals that were intended to keep the gods happy. You'll also look at the typical duties that people in Aztec society had to carry out in their life and try your hand at some delicious Aztec food recipes. Prepare for a fun but gruesome journey!

The Aztec calendar

The Aztec calendar was based on astrological observations of the passage of the Sun, the Moon, and the planets. There was not only one calendar, but two!

1. The 'xiuhpohualli' had 365 days and described the days and rituals relating to the change in seasons. It could also be referred to as the agricultural calendar.
2. The 'tonalpohualli' translates into 'day-count,' and it had only 260 days. It was more commonly known as the sacred calendar.

In everyday life, the Aztec year comprised of 18 months of 20 days each that made up the 'xiuhpohualli' calendar. In addition, there were five 'useless days' called *Nemontemi* when people fasted, abstaining from sexual activities and pleasure. These were also the days when people engaged in voluntary bloodletting to appease the gods.

The calendar was at the heart of the Aztec festivities and events. Many of these are known to us, thanks to the efforts of Diego Durán, a Dominican friar who was born in Spain but arrived in Mexico in the 1540s while he was still a child. As a result, he grew up playing with the Aztec kids and befriended their families who shared more with him than they did with the other priests towards whom they were hostile.

He wrote his three books (one on Aztec history, one on their gods and rites, and another on the ancient calendar) in a desperate attempt to open the eyes of the other priests who funded religious activities in Aztec society. They had no idea that many brutal sacrifices still took place in secret, disguised as the Christian celebrations of the saints. Durán recorded these in detail, upset by most of them. Nonetheless, some of these festivities were rather nice and joyful, bringing the community closer together in a collective celebration.

For example, the first day of each month was a feast day. What's more, each day that started with number '1' in front of it was a day when all the people born under that sign were honoured. If the first day of the month happened to be the day of crocodile, then everyone who was named after the crocodile was honoured on that day.

This is what the Aztec calendar looked like, calculated in Durán's time.

Month and Description	Symbol
Atlcahualo, *Cuauhitlehua* March 1 - 20 Translation: Ceasing of Water, Rising Trees During this month, the Aztec people went around touching plants and offering food for gods, symbolic of them asking for a fruitful year.	
Tlacaxipehualiztli March 21 - April 9 Translation: Rites of Fertility The start of this month marked the spring equinox. One of the most gruesome Aztec rituals took place during this month, in honour of the god Xipe Totec. Captured warriors were sacrificed, their skin flayed and worn by the priests of Xipe Totec for 20 days. Children ran after the priests, playfully hitting them with their wooden toy swords. Gladiatorial battles and military ceremonies also took place during this month.	
Tozoztontli April 10 - 29	

Translation: Little Vigil Several gods were honoured during this month with human sacrifices and offerings of flowers. The deities honoured during this month included Tlaloc, Coatlicue, Chalchihutlicue, and Centeotl. The flayed skins that the priests had worn during the previous month were buried in the Yopico temple.	
Huey Tozoztli April 30 - May 19 Translation: Great Vigil Several gods were honored during this month. These include Centeotl, Chalchiuhtlicue, Xilonen, Chicomecoatl, and Tlaloc. Human sacrifices were rampant again, including child sacrifices and the sacrifice of a maiden as an offering to the corn and earth deities. People worshipped the new corn and asked for blessings over the seed of corn for that year. Houses and altars everywhere were decorated with corn plants. People and priests also engaged in ceremonial bloodletting, as they did during some of the other months.	
Toxcatl May 20 - June 8 Translation: Dryness During this month, the Aztecs engaged in perhaps one of their most bizarre rituals. They chose one person from their midst to represent Tezcatlipoca, the god of fate and destiny. This person would be treated like a god, representing Tezcatlipoca until the day of his sacrifice. During the 17 days of this ceremony, people danced and feasted. The festivities culminated with the sacrifice of the fake Tezcatlipoca, along with small birds.	
Etzalcualiztli June 9 - 28	

Translation: Eating Maize and Beans

This month pretty much did what it says on the tin - people feasted by eating boiled maize and beans during this month's festivities. The celebrations were dedicated to Tlaloc and Chalchiuhtlicue. But the merry festivities were not without their gruesome sacrifices. According to some chronicles, 15 children were sacrificed in the mountains, while others state people who impersonated the god Tlaloc and his wife cohabited for 20 days before they were sacrificed at midnight.

Tecuilhuitontli
June 29 - July 18
Translation: Feast for the Revered Ones

The seventh month in the Aztec calendar celebrated the work of the salt makers and the common folk who were commemorated by the nobles who hosted great festivities in their honour. The concubines of the nobles could leave their houses and walk along the streets with flower crowns on their heads. The Great Speaker would perform a dance in the public and distribute gifts among people. The saltmakers had to dance too - they spent ten entire days, dancing in pairs, holding the end of a robe and singing in a high-pitched tone. The two main gods honored during this month were Xochipilli and Huixtocihuatl.

Huey Tecuilhuitl
July 19 - August 7
Translation: Feast for the Greatly Revered Ones

During this month, corn was usually ripe. Among the festivities, some gruesome sacrifices took place. A virgin was sacrificed during this month, lying on top of four men who made a kind of a table that

supported her, before they were sacrificed too.	
Miccailhuitontli August 8 - 27 Translation: Feast to the Revered Deceased The goddess Mictecacihuatl, or their Lady of the Dead, presided over this month, dedicated to children and the dead. People engaged in joyful festivities and feasting to remember their children and their ancestors who had passed away, and to honor Mictecacihuatl. Food items and small clay figurines or images of the deceased were brought to the altars as an offering.	
Xócotl huetzi, Huey Miccailhuitl August 28 - September 16 Translation: Feast to the Greatly Revered Deceased Continuing the theme of the previous month, the Aztec continued to honour their dead during this month.	
Ochpaniztli September 17 - October 6 Translation: Sweeping and Cleaning This was the month when the grandmother was honoured everywhere. It was also the month of cleaning and sweeping streets, houses, even rivers and streams, similar to our Western practices of 'spring cleaning.' However, Durán had his doubts - he believed that this month encouraged people to be sloths and neglect cleansing practices for the rest of the year.	

Teotleco October 7 - 26 Translation: Return of the Gods On the 12th day of this month, the Aztec people spent the entire night waiting on the priests to announce the birth of their main god. They awaited the birth by practicing severe blood-letting and self-mutilation. When the birth was finally announced, everyone joined in a party, where people cut themselves and, caught in a daze of euphoria, rubbed blood all over each other.	
Tepeilhuitl October 27 - November 15 Translation: Feast of the Mountains During this month, people honoured the volcanoes all around them, especially Popocatepetl. The Aztecs made tiny volcanoes from gemstones and painted faces on them. They honoured the volcanoes with a grand feast and finished the day by chopping off the head of the volcano figurine using a sharp knife.	
Quecholli November 16 - December 5 Translation: Precious Feather One of the four creator gods in the Aztec pantheon was honoured. His name was Mixcoatl, otherwise known as the Cloud Serpent. Associated with the morning star, he also represented the hunt, having features of a deer or rabbit. Thus, a ceremonial hunt marked the festivities during this month. The last day of this month was also the day when the Aztecs made new weapons.	

Panquetzaliztli December 6 - December 25 Translation: Raising the Banners The fifteenth month of the Aztec calendar marked the Winter Solstice that occurred on 21 December. This was an incredibly important day, and preparations were carried out for the entire month. During this month, people decorated their houses with paper flags and trees, similarly to our preparations for Christmas festivities. Except the Aztecs also engaged in human sacrifice, among ritual races, dances, prayers, songs, and processions. People ate little during this month. At the end of the month though, an edible figurine of one of their gods, made of amaranth seeds and honey, was cut into pieces so that everyone could eat their share of the god.	
Atemoztli December 26 - January 14 Translation: Descent of the Water Four days of bloodletting preceded this month, along with a strict fast. The festivities and rituals performed during this month aimed to appease Tlaloc, the Aztec god of water, to send waters down to earth, so they would help sow the season's new corn. The feast held in honour of Tlaloc was attended by the nobles (chiefs and lords). Corresponding rituals that were performed during this month include the sacrifice of slaves in the hills, the drowning of children to appease the rain god, and some gentler rituals, such as offerings of feathers.	
Tititl January 15 - February 12 Translation: Stretching for Growth The planting season began during this month. People only ate amaranth leaves with their usual staple food, corn, as these had a	

special symbolism. The Aztecs also stretched the arms and legs of their children to promote growth. Typically, a boy and a girl were sacrificed to Tlaloc, the god responsible for rain, so he would send rain to the newly planted crops. This is because the tears of children were considered beneficial for summoning rain.	
Izcalli February 4 - 23 Translation: Encouragement for the Land & People The Aztec lived on the cusp of the cosmic order and its potential collapse into chaos. They had the responsibility to keep their gods happy with their many festivals and rituals, to secure a positive outcome for their people. During the month of Izcalli, their efforts culminated in ritual hunts, sacrifice, and a sacred court dance. The entire month was devoted to fire.	
Nemontemi February 24 - 28 Translation: Empty or Useless Days As opposed to the neighboring Mayan cultures, who saw these five additional days as a dangerous period, when the worlds between the dead and the living merged, the Aztecs simply saw these last five days as useless. Instead of doing any special rituals to protect themselves from the dead, as the Maya did, they fasted, abstained from pleasures, such as sexual activity, and generally felt displeased during this time, wishing for the five days to be over soon.	

The Aztec language

The Aztecs called themselves the Mexica, and they spoke Náhuatl. This language belongs to the Uto-Aztecan family tree and was spoken by the Aztec and the Toltec civilization. Since the Aztecs dominated most of the Valley of Mexico during the peak of their civilization, most of the tribes in their kingdom spoke the language.

Later, during the 16th and 17th centuries, Náhuatl also became a literary language, as many important poetic and historical works, including chronicles and administrative documents, were written down in Náhuatl.

Today, the language is still spoken in the regions of central and western Mexico by an estimated 1.5 million people. What's more, many of the words we used in our everyday language have been taken from Náhuatl. Here are some of them.

Hint: These words describe food items, animals, and plants that the Spanish conquistadors encountered for the first time when they discovered the New World. Thus, they absorbed these unfamiliar words into Spanish, as they did not have a better way to describe the exotic things they'd seen.

1. A hot, spicy plant often used to prepare Mexican meals.
   C _ _ _ i
2. A nutritious green-skinned fruit, rich in Vitamin B and K.
   A _ _ _ _ _ o
3. A wolf-like dog, also called prairie wolf, found mostly in North America.
   C _ _ _ _ e
4. A kind of sauce or condiment, made with mashed avocado, chopped onion, tomatoes, and chili peppers. Great with tacos!
   G _ _ _ _ _ _ _ e
5. A species of wild cat, found in South America.
   O _ _ _ _ t

The Aztec laws and social roles

Aztec daily life was steeped in religious ritual. People also had to 'pay their dues' to their community by setting a prime example, and the nobles were more accountable than commoners on this.

The adults within Aztec society were expected to take care of their children as well as their elders. Only when an Aztec citizen reached the ripe old age of 52 could they live as they wanted to. Elders were often seen drunk in public, and no one raised an eyebrow. By this time, they'd successfully completed their duties, and they no longer owed anything to the society they lived in. In other words, they had retired, and many laws no longer applied to them.

The commoners gave birth to their children at home, in the sweat-baths or *temazcals*. A midwife helped deliver the baby, and she'd stay with the family for a few days, helping the new mother settle into her new role. On the fourth day, the baby was brought into the courtyard to greet the curious neighbours, and bathed in a tub of lake reeds. Three boys would call out the baby's new name - this name was chosen by the midwife, and it was only temporary. The official name was given to them during one of the festivals in May by a priest from the temple.

Only the nobles could choose cool names for their offspring. For example, their king Moctezuma received the great name of 'angry lord.' The day you were born determined your name and destiny. For example, you could be called 'five eagle' or 'two earthquake.' People born on the day of the wind, for example, were considered to be lazy and distracted, drifting around from place to place like the wind.

Each day was governed by a different deity who was responsible for distributing the life energy, or *tonalli,* that the Aztecs believed flowed through every human being. In no particular order, here are some of the days and what it meant if you were born on this day.

 Cipactli - the day of the crocodile or dragon.

This day is governed by Tonacatecuhtli, the Lord of Nurturance, according to the Aztec calendar. This day was considered auspicious and signified both honour and advancement to the person born on this day. Energy and work would lead to rewards and recognition later in life.

 Cōātl - the day of the serpent.

The day of the Serpent is governed by Chalchihuitlicue. This day was considered as the day of the snaking river that always changes on its own effort without changing. This is symbolic of the fleeting moments, caught in the drift of eternal water. The day of the snake was considered a bad day for acting on self-interests or selfish gains, as the day was reserved for humility.

 Ōcēlōtl - the day of the jaguar.

The day of the Jaguar is governed by Tlazolteotl who provided *tonalli* for people born on this day. This was a good day for battle, signifying valour and the right amount of recklessness. This day honoured warriors who sacrificed their lives in the name of others.

If you want to find out the Aztec meaning of your birthday, you can check out this website: https://www.azteccalendar.com/

What happened to your umbilical cord?

Burying their baby's umbilical cord was an important ritual to the Aztecs that tied them to their homes. The umbilical cord of a newborn was buried outside their home. For boys, it was buried under a miniature shield and bow. For girls, it was buried under a grinding stone. This was symbolic to their roots in this home, that would remain there forever, connecting them to their family and ancestry.

Childhood wasn't fun and games for the Aztec kids - at age five, the children of commoners were already hard at work, either doing more physical work if they were boys or helping around the house and cleaning, if they were girls. They soon started school, and following graduation, the boys were enlisted in the army as part of their obligatory service. Their worth as a man was determined not by how many poems they'd written or how beautifully they could sing (all skills they learned at school) but by how many captives they brought back home with them.

The wedding day

People couldn't choose whom they could marry in Aztec society - their relatives and teachers decided on the most suitable life partner for them. Men married by age of 20 while girls were married off at a much younger age - between 10 to 12 years of age.

The wedding day wasn't yours to choose either - it was done by the soothsayers who chose the best possible day for a long and happy marriage. The ceremony took place at the bride's home where guests were served in order of importance (parents and grandparents of the bride and groom were served first, relatives next, and so on). After the wedding feast, the bride was the bathed and dressed at sunset, following which she received something of a lecture from the groom's parents - they reminded her that she was now an adult, and that she must part with her childish age (even though she may have only been 10 years old). The young and indoctrinated bride was then carried over to the groom's house, followed by a procession of the family members, all carrying torches.

Inside the groom's house, the couple sat on a mat, where their robes were tied together, signifying their bond in marriage. (In fact, these ceremonial wedding mats can still be seen in some bridal shops in Mexico and other parts of Latin America to this day). The elders hastily left the house, burning incense in their wake, as they left the couple to enjoy some privacy.

Since they were now adults, they were expected to take care of their elders, allowing them to live with the rest of the family. They also had to carry out their duties at work and care for their children. In fact, raising their children to be good citizens was of utmost importance in Aztec society. All their efforts and finances went toward supporting their children.

Everything the Aztecs did was done only if the priests said so. If the priests believed that a particular day was bad for farming, then no farming was done on that day.

Aside from being farmers, craftsmen, or artisans, the men from the common rank were also warriors, if a time of need arrived. If they were summoned to battle, they had to abandon their homes and go.

Perhaps it's not surprising people finally let loose in their 50s. They no longer had the burden of setting a good public example. The old men no longer needed to go to war, and they could do whatever they liked without any judgment.

The typical diet of an Aztec citizen

While most Aztec diets consisted of maize (or corn), beans and squash, three types of crop that were often grown together across Mesoamerica, your diet varied according to your social rank in society. Everyone enjoyed the occasional fish, rabbit, armadillo, snake, wild turkey or coyote. A commoner or a slave in Tenochtitlán probably enjoyed a better diet than a person of the same rank in Europe.

In addition, people of the Aztec Empire also ate chilies, tomatoes, limes, cashews, sweet potatoes, and peanuts, which was only later introduced in Europe. They also domesticated some animals and insects for food - these included bees, turkeys, and ducks. They also domesticated dogs.

On the gross spectrum, they also ate grasshoppers, iguanas, snakes, and worms, although in minimal amounts. They knew how to make bread and cheese type foods, utilizing a type of algae that grew in the Texcoco lake water.

The Aztec also drank a thick drink called chocolate. The Aztec only drank sugar-free chocolate because they didn't have sugar. They also spiced up their thick chocolate drink by adding peppers, processed corn, and spices. They serve a similar drink in Mexico called atole.

The cocoa bean was so important and treasured that it was used as currency in the markets. The Aztecs believed their god Quetzalcoatl brought them the cocoa bean, after having attained it from the tree of life.

Three delicious Aztec recipes for a healthy Aztec feast!

The cuisine the Aztecs ate would have been different to what we can produce today, but many foods in Mexico have Aztec influences. The Aztecs did not use fat in their cooking but still produced some mouth-watering dishes. Here is our pick of the three best Aztec recipes

Starter - Aztec Tortilla soup

This lovely Aztec Tortilla soup is sure to get your guests' taste buds going. The best part is that you can use stale tortillas for the recipe and they'll taste just as delicious as if they were fresh. This recipe has been 'borrowed' and adapted from Albatz blog. It serves two to four people. You can find the full recipe at http://blogs.ubc.ca/albatz/2012/10/04/eat-like-an-aztec-tortilla-soup-recipe

What you'll need:

- 4 to 8 corn tortillas;
- 1 medium onion;
- 2 garlic cloves;
- 4 or 5 ripe tomatoes;
- 6 cups chicken broth;
- 2 sprigs of epazote;
- salt and pepper for seasoning.

1. Brush the tortillas lightly with corn oil, slice in strips and bake in the oven until crispy.
2. Chop and fry the onion lightly in a little corn oil. Mash the two garlic cloves. Blanch, skin, or grind the tomatoes (alternatively, you can substitute a tin of stewed tomatoes instead) and mash everything together in a saucepan. Add the chicken broth to the stew, along with the epazote. Season and salt to taste.

And if you wanted to give your Aztec soup a fancy finish, you can try adding a couple of avocados, sliced into cubes straight into the soup or on the side, along with some cream cheese and fresh limes. And if you want your tortilla soup to have that Aztec kick, toss in a couple of dried pasilla chilies!

Main course - Aztec chicken

This scrumptious and easy Aztec chicken recipe is sure to hit the spot, even for the hungriest of diners! It serves four people, and you can change some of the ingredients to suit their tastes. The original recipe can be found on the Food Network website that can be accessed via this link http://www.foodnetwork.co.uk/recipes/aztec-chicken.html

What you'll need:

- 6 chicken breast fillets;
- 140g seasoned plain flour;
- 1 egg
- 240ml double cream;
- 240ml olive oil;
- 12 large raw prawns;
- 3 garlic cloves;
- 6 pepperoncini;

- 170g streaky bacon;
- 180ml rum;
- 700ml chicken stock;
- 1 avocado;
- salt and pepper for seasoning.

1. Rub the chicken breasts with some seasoned flour. Crack the eggs into a separate bowl and mix in the cream. Coat the chicken breasts in the egg mixture, so it creates a nice coating. Cook for a few minutes in a saucepan, until the fillets, have turned a lovely golden brown colour and the meat has thoroughly cooked.

2. Add some oil to another saucepan and heat until hot. Drain the excess mixture from the chicken breasts and place them on the frying pan. Now fry the prawns for just a moment, and when they seem halfway done, stir in the crushed garlic, pepperoncini, and chopped bacon.

3. Once you've taken the saucepan off the heat, it's time to add some rum! Pour over your concoction, and light it up with a long match (remember, safety first) and wait for the flames to subside. Add the chicken stock, put the saucepan back on heat and season with salt and pepper to taste. Once it's been frying for a moment, remove ⅓ of the stock and add some avocado. Reduce the heat until the mixture has the consistency of a glaze.

Voila! Your Aztec-worthy main course is ready to be served - place the chicken breasts on a plate, stack the prawns on top and drizzle your delicious glaze over the top.

Dessert - Aztec Hot Chocolate

What could top the delicious taste of a thick, delicious hot chocolate drink! It's like having a hug in a mug. This recipe has been adapted from the Time Traveler Kids website, which can be accessed here http://timetravellerkids.co.uk/news/how-to-make-aztec-hot-chocolate/

This recipe could serve anywhere between two to four people, depending on how thirsty they are for some Aztec chocolate!

What you'll need:

- 50g dark chocolate (no sugar allowed);
- a few drops vanilla extract;
- just a pinch of cinnamon and cayenne pepper to spice things up.

1. Break up the chocolate into small squares and place it in a clean saucepan. Pour 300ml of boiling water inside and watch as the chocolate melts. Before it has fully dissolved, add the vanilla extract, cinnamon, and cayenne pepper.

Your chocolate is ready to be served!

Chapter 8 – The Fall of Tenochtitlán

To begin the story of the fall of Tenochtitlán, another story needs to be told. This is the story of one of Mesoamerica's most important gods, Quetzalcóatl ("The Feathered Serpent"). As the name suggests, this god was a serpent with feathers.

Although other Mesoamerican cultures, like the Maya, knew Quetzalcóatl by a different name, most agreed he presided over the rain and winds, and he was also the creator of mankind, and later the creator of the cosmos, along with his brothers Huitzilopochtli and Tezcatlipoca. From 1200 AD onwards, Quetzalcóatl was revered as the patron god of priesthood, learning, science, the arts, and agriculture. Among Quetzalcóatl's inventions were the calendar and the discovery of corn and maize.

Now, we come to a point in the story where, once again, you must make up your own mind as to which side you wish to believe. Most of the material within this chapter comes from the autobiography of Bernal Díaz del Castillo, one of the Spanish conquistadors who wrote his work The True History of the Conquest of New Spain at an old age, many years after the conquest. Although Díaz witnessed every battle for himself and he displayed respect for the locals, he was nonetheless a Spanish soldier who, to some extent, idealised his leader Hernando Cortés. His work is a great adventure story.

In his work, he introduces the idea that, following many successful battles that the Spanish fought against the local tribes before they got to Tenochtitlán, the locals began regarding them as gods. Later, Moctezuma II welcomed the Spaniards in his great city, greeting Cortés as the returning incarnation of Quetzalcóatl. Whether this is true remains debatable. It is certainly one version of the truth - the natives may have had another.

How did the Spaniards get to Tenochtitlán? How did they conquer the vast Aztec empire with only a few hundred soldiers?

The first contact with Europe

Hernando Cortés was not only a brilliant warrior and strategist, he was also an ambitious man and an excellent orator, and this ability saved him on many occasions during the conquest. He landed on the shores of Mesoamerica in 1519 with only 11 ships, 500 men, 13 horses, and a small number of cannon, ignoring the orders of his former patrón Diego Velázquez de Collar who decided to cancel his mission at the last moment. Upon landing in Yucatan, which was Mayan territory at the time, he established a settlement (now called Veracruz).

A portrait of Hernando Cortés. Source: https://en.wikipedia.org/wiki/Hern%C3%A1n_Cort%C3%A9s

Aside from his troops, Cortés was aided by two important people on his conquest. First, he met Geronimo de Aguilar, a Franciscan priest who'd survived a shipwreck and escaped captivity. Aguilar had learned the local language and became a translator for Cortés. He later met La Malinche or Doña Marina (as she was called by the Spanish), a beautiful indigenous woman who was given to Cortés as a captive. But instead of being his slave, Doña Marina became an important adviser and interpreter (who spoke both Mayan and Náhuatl) during the conquest, and Cortés' mistress, who later gave birth to his son Martín, one of the first 'Mestizos' (people of Native American and European descent).

The road to Tenochtitlán

From the natives Cortés and his crew encountered along the way, he learned of the great wealth of the Aztecs. The Spanish were thirsty for gold, but the Aztecs didn't hold gold in high esteem. Moctezuma II, having found out about their obsession, sent gold to the Spanish, along with jade jewels and feathers and a message that the king welcomed them, but would only continue to send presents if they stayed away from Tenochtitlán.

While the Spanish were getting closer and closer, Moctezuma II was plagued by a prophecy he'd received from an allied ruler – that enemies would come from the East and this would mark the end of the Aztec empire. According to some accounts, this coincided with the Aztec calendar prophecies that Quetzalcóatl would return in the same year. Whether Moctezuma II really believed that the Spanish were, gods remain open for speculation.

The success of the Spanish conquest was a combination of military force, excellent leadership, and their two trusted interpreters. However, an even more significant role was played by the locals' hostility toward the Aztecs. This is because the Aztecs, a powerful military force, often treated their subjects harshly, asking them to pay steep tributes, and sending their armies to deal with those who refused to pay.

Although at first, they regarded Cortés with suspicion and hostility, the Totonacs and Tlaxcalans eventually joined forces with the Spanish and marched jointly towards Tenochtitlán. In addition, Cortés managed to convince the soldiers sent by his opponents in Europe to join their army on a conquest that the world would never forget. This earned him the loyalty of 400 men, to add to his own army of over 400 men and the support of 2,000 Totonac warriors.

Although many of the locals joined Cortés on his quest, not everything he said went down well. Upon witnessing the acts of human sacrifice, a widespread practice across Mesoamerica, as well as seeing acts of cannibalism and sodomy, Cortés made continuous attempts to educate the locals to stop these practices. In response, the locals were greatly offended, saying they had to do this to appease their gods. They regarded these ideas as insults to their deities. This clash of perception would later play a significant role in the conquest of Tenochtitlán, but more on that later.

The gracious welcome

When Moctezuma II heard about the advances made by the Spanish, he employed several tactics in how to deal with them. As already mentioned, he started by sending them gifts. As the Spanish advanced further and made more allies, they hid thousands of Aztec warriors in one of the cities along the way, but thanks to his informants, Cortés found out about this in time and sacked the city. Moctezuma II sent more messages his way, blaming the locals for conspiring against the Spanish. He finally invited the conquistadors to visit his city. Perhaps this was an act of caution, or perhaps Moctezuma II had surrendered to the fate predicted by the prophecy. Either way, on 8 November 1519 he allowed the Spanish and their indigenous allies to march inside the Aztec capital. Led by Cortés, their entourage entered the city using Iztapalapa, a causeway associated with their god Quetzalcóatl. It was covered in flowers, as Moctezuma II, dressed in fine silks and adorned with feathers and jewels, gave the Spanish a warm and gracious welcome.

He bowed to the Spanish and, according to Bernardino de Sahagún, Florentine Codex, Book 12, Chapter 16, this is what he said in his welcome speech. As you read this, be aware that this again is just one version of the truth.

"Our Lord (..) you have come here to sit on your throne, to sit under its canopy, which I have kept for awhile for you. For the rulers and governors [of past times] have gone: Itzcoatl, Moctezuma I, Axayacatl, Tiçocic, and Ahuitzotl. [Since they are gone], your poor vassal has been in charge for you, to govern the city of Mexico. Will they come back to the place of their absence? If even one came, he might witness the marvel that has taken place in my time, see what I am seeing, as the only descendant of our lords. For I am not just dreaming, not just sleepwalking, not seeing you in my dreams. I am not just dreaming that I have seen you and have looked at you face to face. I have been worried for a long time, looking toward the unknown from which you have come, the mysterious place. For our rulers departed, saying that you would come to your city and sit upon your throne. And now it has been fulfilled; you have returned. Go enjoy your palace, rest your body. Welcome our lords to this land."

And with those words, Moctezuma II led the amazed conquistadors inside his palace where they were made to feel welcome and honoured, treated like gods indeed.

The captive king

The Spanish were welcomed with feasts and tours around the city. They enjoyed all its marvels, and they felt equally amazed and repelled by the city's many practices. Every day they were treated to incredible dance shows, feasts, and human sacrifices. Again, they asked the Aztecs to stop doing what they were doing, that their Christian god disapproved of this, and this created tensions between the Aztecs and the conquistadors (not everyone was as friendly toward them as the king).

Tensions soon built up between the Aztecs and the conquistadors. Although Moctezuma II was urged by his brother Cuitlahuac and nephew Cacamatzin to act against the Spanish, he refuted them. Although plenty of men in his council disagreed with the opinion of their king, Moctezuma II was nonetheless their ruler, and his word was final. It is unclear why he took such a passive stance, but the price he paid was fatal. On 14 November, only a few days after the arrival of the Spanish, Moctezuma II was taken hostage in his palace. Allegedly, it was a peaceful surrender, and the king aided the Spanish conquest from then on. According to some accounts, he became friends with Cortés, sharing long conversations and enjoying board games together.

He allowed the Spanish to remain in his palace and ordered a large tribute of gold and precious gifts to be collected for them. Slowly, the Aztecs started to doubt their own king and turn against him. Tensions escalated at a feast that the Aztecs held in the name of the Spanish.

Massacre at the festival of Tóxcatl

Word reached Cortés that his former patron Velázquez was plotting against him. He sent a force of 19 ships, loaded with more than 800 soldiers, 80 horsemen, 120 crossbowmen and 80 arquebusiers to capture Cortés. The army was led by Pánfilo de Narváez, who was ordered to return Cortés back to Cuba where he would be tried.

When Cortés received the news, he quickly assembled a force of 240 men and left Tenochtitlán to repel Narváez's forces. He ambushed Narváez's camp late at night, leaving him imprisoned in

Veracruz. And what of Narváez's army? Cortés used his orator's talent to charm them with tales of the great Aztec wealth, so they joined his forces and followed him back to the Aztec capital.

Meanwhile, the man whom Cortés had left in command, Pedro de Alvarado, was invited to a feast dedicated to their god Tezcatlipoca. Moctezuma II had attained permission from both Cortés and Alvarado to hold a festival in the honour of this Aztec deity. Alvarado had one condition though - no human sacrifice was allowed. However, the Aztecs had spent a long time preparing to sacrifice a young man who'd impersonated the god Toxcatl for an entire year. Without human sacrifice, their festival was no festival at all!

Alvarado became more suspicious of the Aztecs and ordered the torture of their priests and nobles, who revealed to him the Aztec were planning a revolt. He allowed the festival to commence in the Patio of Dances just outside their great temple. As the dancing grew more euphoric, Alvarado became more agitated. Seeing people feasting on the flesh of other men was the last straw. He went berserk. Alvarado ordered all the gates to be closed and slaughtered everyone on scene - men, women, and children.

While Díaz does not make much of this, the native accounts describe this as a horror they'd never seen before. From their perspective, they were simply celebrating the best of Aztec culture - for them, the festival was filled with beauty and sacredness - and the act of the Spanish was complete sacrilege to their values. A revolt followed, with thousands of Aztecs attacking the conquistadors. They even turned on their own king, who was instructed to give a speech to calm the angry masses.

Once he found out about the events, Cortés hurried back. The roads were shut, and the causeways were drawn or burnt down, so it was difficult for Cortés' forces to get back inside the capital. The Aztecs had stopped supplying the Spanish with food and gifts, disobeying the orders of their king. Just like they'd turned against their king, they now turned against each other, killing those whom they suspected as helping the conquistadors. In one final attempt to restore peace and initiate negotiations, Cortés sent Moctezuma II to give a speech to the maddening crowd. While he spoke, he was hit by a rock and died shortly thereafter. It is said that both Aztecs and the Spanish conquistadors wept over his death. Moctezuma's younger brother Cuitláhuac was elected as the next ruler of the Aztecs.

The Night of Sorrows
"La Noche Triste" or The Night of Sorrows is the name given to the events that followed when the Spanish tried to escape Tenochtitlán on 1 July 1520. Although he risked looking weak in front of the Aztecs and his native allies, Cortés really had no choice but to escape the city. Although they had gathered about 42,000 tons of gold, they could only carry so much with them. The Spanish built platforms from the doors within their compound and lay them across the gaps in causeways,

before loading them with gold. This proved to be a disaster, and many of them were captured by the Aztecs. Some drowned in the lake, weighed down by the weight of the gold, while others were captured by the angry Aztecs and dragged to the top of Templo Mayor, where their screams echoed and pierced the ears of Cortés. He lost a third of his army that night, and he is said to have wept under a tree later that night, grieving the loss of so many men.

The Spanish regroup and form alliances

The Spanish found refuge in their allies from Tlacopan. They were headed towards Tlaxcala, chased all the way by the Aztecs. The conquistadors defeated the Aztecs at the Battle of Otumba, but only just. A vital role was played by the shock value of seeing caballeros, or knights on horseback. Five days later, Cortés finally reached Tlaxcala. His losses amounted to 860 Spanish soldiers, more than 1,000 Tlaxcalans, and many Spanish women who had accompanied Narváez. One of Moctezuma II's daughters died as well, leaving behind an infant by Cortés.

Lucky for Cortés, the Tlaxcalans hated the Aztecs so much they became powerful allies of the Spanish. They asked for expensive tributes in return, which Cortés promised. Other allies included the Huexotzinco, Atlixco, Tliliuhqui-Tepecs, Tetzcocans, Chalca, Alcohua and the Tepanecs. Tetzcoco that had been previously allied with Tenochtitlán also joined the Spanish and turned against the Aztecs.

But the Spanish became divided too. Many of the troops wished for nothing more than to return to Veracruz after all they'd been through. But for Cortés, this would mean eventually being captured and convicted as a traitor of the King of Spain. So, he gave another one of his convincing speeches and eventually got his troops to agree to his quest, marching on Tenochtitlán once again. Unknown to them, the Spanish had another powerful ally that killed more people than anyone else - infectious diseases.

The defeat of Tenochtitlán

Smallpox played a crucial role in defeating the Aztecs. In October 1520, an epidemic of smallpox broke out in Tenochtitlán. It was a disease that the Aztecs had not encountered before, probably introduced by one of the slaves from Narváez's ships. The disease raged in the Aztec capital for some 60 days, leading to famine as the local farmers were too sick to tend to their crops. It must be said that the Spanish also suffered losses due to the disease; however, these were less dire than those suffered by the Aztecs. Within a year, almost 40% of the Aztec population had died, including their leader Cuitlahuac, without any effort on the Spanish part.

Although Moctezuma II is often associated with being the last leader of the Aztecs, Cuauhtemoc was their final king. He was elected in February 1521. Weakened by the diseases and still in the process of mourning their dead, the Aztecs stayed within the walls of their once-great city, hoping, wishing, and praying to their gods that the Spanish had gone for good.

But the Spanish were going nowhere. Having regrouped and rounded up their allies, they marched on Tenochtitlán once more. The decisive battle for Tenochtitlán took place between 22 May and 13 August 1521. It was a ninety-three-day siege that Cortés began by ordering an army to guard the entrance to each causeway. By this time, he had a massive army, consisting of his own seasoned men and more than 30,000 native allies. His next step was to cut the aqueducts and prevent a fresh-water supply to the city. Many battles took place during this time, and the Aztecs were victorious in some while defeated in others. Some of the battles were fought along the huge causeways, and the Aztecs used tactics like shooting arrows from canoes to repel the Spanish. Overwhelmed by their force, the Aztec leader Cuauhtemoc decided to escape but was subsequently captured by the Spanish. This led to the Aztec surrender on 13 August 1521.

The future of Tenochtitlán

Following his successful victory, Cortés was recognised as governor and captain-general of New Spain in 1523. The last leader of the Aztecs, Cuauhtemoc, was hanged in 1524 in Chiapas.

However, Cortés was degraded to the position of a civil governor and forced to return to Spain, as the King of Spain feared that he was becoming a tad too powerful. And that was understandable since Cortés had been in charge of an empire containing 500 small city-states with a total population of 6,000,000 indigenous people. He built a new city on the ruins of Tenochtitlán, known today as Mexico City.

Cortés returned to Central America, searching for a route from the Atlantic to the Pacific. He failed in his search, but instead, he found California. He died in 1547, after spending six years on an estate in Seville, allegedly a bitter man.

Conclusion

The ancient Aztecs, along with other Mesoamerican civilizations, were fierce warriors who wanted to attain higher levels of consciousness. For all the wonders of their culture, their tradition of human sacrifice, which they didn't see as a particularly evil practice, horrified the Spanish conquistadors, and gave them a means to justify their conquest. But which party was morally right?

It seems that neither side could perceive the perspective of the other, and neither was interested in doing so. The Spanish condemned the Aztec sacrifices and the Aztecs, in turn, condemned the Spanish for insulting their gods. Greed played a significant role for both parties. Yes, the conquistadors were thirsty for gold, and this cost them many men, but the Aztecs may not have been defeated had it not been for their former allies turning against them, sick and tired of paying so much tribute and taxes to their Aztec overlords.

So, what are we to make of their legacy today, when a new city stands on the rubble of the old world? Who are the people, living in Mexico today? Are they Aztec or Spanish?

It seems the memorial dedicated to three horrific events in the history of Mexico says it best. The Plaza of Three Cultures in Mexico City commemorates the final Battle of Tenochtitlán in 1521, the violent protests of 1968, and the devastating 1985 earthquake.

The Plaza of Three Cultures in Mexico City is also a tribute to the two cultures that clashed (the Spanish and the Aztecs), to eventually give a painful birth to the new culture that inhabits Mexico today - the modern *Mestizo*.

Completed in 1964, the Plaza of Three Cultures is in the exact location where 40,000 Aztecs are said to have died in their final attempt to defend their once-great city. The inscription in the Plaza gives the following account of the conquest of New Spain: "Neither a victory nor a defeat, but the painful moment of birth of the Mexico of today, of a race of *Mestizos*."

Can you help?

If you enjoyed this particular part on the Aztecs, then it would be really appreciated it if you would post a short review for the book on Amazon.

Thanks for your support!

Part 3: Incas

A Captivating Guide to the History of the Inca Empire and Civilization

Introduction

One of the most notable ancient cultures of South America is undoubtedly the Inca Civilization. They once ruled over the largest empire in South America. Not only that - their empire was also the largest in the world at the time.

However, it didn't last long - within about a hundred years, the empire that stretched all the way from modern-day Quito, Ecuador in the north to modern Santiago, Chile in the south, lay in ruin. The Inca Empire that ruled over 10 million subjects was conquered by a few hundred Spanish conquistadors in the mid-16th century.

Despite its grand appearances, the Inca empire turned out to be weak and quickly disintegrated when the Spanish conquistadors arrived on their shores, with a measly force of 168 men, their leader Francisco Pizarro among them. How was this possible?

But there are many more mysteries surrounding the Incas. Where did the Incas originate? And how did they come to rule over their vast empire that incorporated mountaintops, tropical jungles, and coastal lands? What were the most notable achievements of their great kings? What did their temples and monuments look like, especially the capital city of Cusco and their breath-taking mountaintop settlement at Machu Picchu in modern-day Peru?

In this book, we'll discover what the Incas had for lunch, how their society was structured and their ideas about Cosmology and the origins of our world.

But before we embark on this journey of discovery, it's important to understand that the history of the Inca empire is not straightforward. The Incas did not have a linear concept of time. They were great orators though, and used stories to pass down oral history to their descendents. Therefore, most of their historical accounts come from Spanish sources or locals who learned Spanish and told the history of the Incas after the conquest.

Each chronicler had their motives and reasons for writing their story - some were seeking to get published, others wanted to justify the Spanish conquest, while others tried to portray the Inca empire as 'the golden age'. The Inca empire could be anything - a brutal totalitarian state that exploited its subjects, an organised system of rigid social structures, or a beautiful utopia.

We'll look at some accredited sources, specifically the work of one of the world's leading experts on Inca civilization Terence N. D'Altroy, Loubat Professor of American Archaeology in the Department of Anthropology and founding Director of the Center for Archaeology at Columbia University in the City of New York.

Chapter 1 – How the Incas Recorded Their History

For the Incas, the stories of their origins are so entangled with their myths and fables that it is difficult to discern fact from fiction. What's more, the Incas revered cosmology and the celestial bodies. Thus, many of their myths are better explained in relation to the movement of the planets, rather than the movement of people.

How the Incas recorded their history

Although they were one of the most sophisticated and advanced civilizations the Spanish Conquistadors encountered, they never developed writing.

<u>Oral storytelling</u>

The Incas had a particular class of individuals whose only duty was to memorise important events from the Inca history, recount them orally at courts or special events, and pass them onto the next generation. There were several issues with this. For example, the storyteller could omit or deliberately include specific events that happened to the previous Inca emperors, depending on whom he happened to be speaking to. What's more, these accounts usually detailed events from the lives of royalty, not the common folk.

Another problem for creating a chronological record of the history of the Incas, including the very beginnings of their civilization, was the Incas did not have a linear view of time. The chronicler and Jesuit missionary Padre Bernabé Cobo recorded the problems that arose when trying to construct a chronological history of the Incas in his book on the history of the Inca Empire.

> When they are asked about things of the past, if something happened more than four to six years ago, what they usually answer is that the incident occurred *ñaupapacha* which means 'a long time ago'; and they give the same answer for events of 20 years back, as for events

of 100 or 1000 years back, except that when the thing is very ancient, they express this by a certain accent and ponderation of their words.

It is therefore difficult to ascertain any linear narrative from the oral history.

Quipus

Quipus were sets of knotted strings that helped the Incas communicate information and deal with numbers with remarkable precision and accuracy. What's more, this device was highly portable so that accurate records could be carried from place to place. The Incas used a variety of colours, strings and different types of knots tied at various ways and lengths to record and communicate important dates, accounts, and statistics. It was even used to record important episodes from folk tales, mythology, and poetry.

How did *quipus* record time and history?

The largest quipus ever found have as many as 1,500 strings of different colours, containing a number of knots that each held its specific meaning. As the method developed, a group of *quipu* masters or *quipucamayos* emerged. Their task was to memorise and keep an oral account that explained a particular *quipu*. This job was passed down from generation to generation. It wasn't an easy task; errors resulted in severe punishments.

Despite the sophistication, the materials used were simple - one needed to get some cotton or wool string and sometimes a wooden bar, from which the strings would hang. The strings had different colours. Each knot was thoughtfully placed in a designated spot. It was the combination of knots, colours and the length of each string that carried a particular meaning.

The method was based on a decimal positional system, counting as far as 10,000. Remarkably, this decimal system closely resembles that which we use in mathematics today. A knot could indicate a number if you counted the turns of the string within it. A knot tied in a figure-of-eight could indicate a fixed value, whereas a string that was missing a knot signified zero. There was also a way to suggest 'secondary strings' that meant this string was an exception or less important than the others.

You could tell what units were used on each *quipu* by looking at the strings placed furthest away from the primary string - this was the key to breaking the code of that particular *quipu*.

So, the Inca creation myth was perpetuated using oral storytelling and *quipus*.

The Spanish chroniclers

Later the history of the Inca and their myths were recorded by the Spanish chroniclers, each of whom had their own agenda, representing the stories in a different light. Many believed the Inca myths and beliefs to be a form of heresy for the Christian faith, and the judgement that the Spaniards imparted when presenting the native accounts resulted in historical inaccuracies.

Some years after the conquest, the Spanish chroniclers started to interview the local Andean people to get a better picture of their past. However, by this time much of their history was skewed towards a biased 'golden era' representation of the Inca rule. This is because the conditions that the locals endure under the Spanish rule were so catastrophic, compared to the treatment they'd received from the Inca rulers.

The first fifty to one hundred years of the Spanish rule are remembered as a 'black time' for the native people of the Andes. The Spanish continued to rage war against the last surviving Inca rulers, as well as fighting each other in a quest for more wealth and power. This left the locals in a difficult position, always torn between the military attacks of the surviving Incas and the Spanish conquistadors with no support from a united, consistent government. Even after the last indigenous Inca ruler Túpac Amaru was decapitated in 1572, the internal conflicts among the Spanish continued, shunned by the King of Spain. Within forty years of the initial Spanish appearance, the local population of the Inca empire had fallen by 50%, with the coastal population suffering the most. A combination of civil wars, forced labour and pestilence that raged for almost one hundred years, made the locals crave for a 'golden age' of the Inca rule and idealise it.

Here are some of the most notable Spanish chroniclers where much of our knowledge of the Incas today comes from:

- Juan de Betanzos's *Narrative of the Incas* (written in the 1550s).

- Bernabé Cobo's *History of the Inca Empire* (1653).

- Garcilaso de la Vega's *El Inca, Royal Commentaries of the Incas, and General History of Peru (*1609).

- Felipe Guaman Poma de Ayala's *El primer nueva corónica y buen gobierno* (written around 1615).

Chapter 2 - The Inca Creation Myth

Similar to other cultures that existed in South America, there was a creator god who created several tribes. The Incas called him Viracocha Pachayachachi, which means 'The Creator of all things.' The Incas believed Viracocha emerged from the waters at Lake Titicaca, creating the earth and the sky before he returned to the waters.

While the age of darkness still ruled over the Earth, he fashioned his first creation - giants made from stone and rocks and gave them special orders that had to be revered.

The Great Flood

But things didn't go as smoothly as Viracocha had planned. The people he'd created kept his orders for a while. After some time though, vice and pride crept among the hearts of the men he'd created, and they stopped following the creator god's orders, preferring to do as they pleased.

As a result, Viracocha cursed them - he turned some of them into stone and other things, and ordered the earth and the sea to swallow the others. Similar to many other creation stories, a great flood swallowed up the earth, known as *uñu pachacuti* or 'water that overturns the land.'

According to some versions, it rained for 60 days and 60 nights, drowning all creation. Some of the giants that were turned back to stone could be seen at sites like Tiahuanaco (or Tiwanaku) and Pukará. Some of the nations are said to have survived, saved from the flood to create the next generation of men.

The second attempt of creation

Viracocha then made a second attempt at creation of man. Still, in the age of darkness, he created people, fashioning them out of clay. He gave them language, agriculture, the arts, and clothes, after which he created all kinds of animals. He told these first people (known as *Vari Viracocharuna)* to populate all corners of the world, but he left them to live inside the Earth.

Viracocha also decided to create the celestial bodies, such as the Sun, the Moon and the stars to bring the world out of the age of darkness and bestow light upon men and all living beings. He used the islands in Lake Titicaca to fashion these heavenly bodies.

Viracocha decided to create another group of men, called *viracochas*. He made these people memorise all the different characteristics of the races and cultures of people that would later populate the world. He sent all the *viracochas* out of the womb of the Earth, leaving two behind. The ones who left, went to all kinds of habitats - caves, streams, rivers, waterfalls - each making the place their home, as Viracocha had ordered them. When they arrived in each settlement, they instructed the people who already lived there that it was time to emerge from the depths of the Earth.

Viracocha ordered all the men to populate every corner of the world, and to live without quarrels, in perfect harmony with each other. He also ordered them to serve him and observe a specific covenant they were not to break, lest they are confounded.

Satisfied, Viracocha spoke to the two people who'd remained and asked them to go forth and help him spread the new civilization far and wide. One of them ventured eastward to Andesuyo, and the other went west, to a region known as Condesuyo. They were instructed to awaken the people they'd meet on their way.

The journey of Viracocha

As for Viracocha, he went towards the great city of Cuzco, dressed in beggar's clothes. He took on different names, such as Con Ticci Viracocha, Atun-Viracocha, and Contiti Viracocha Pachayachachic. He travelled the world, imparting valuable knowledge about the arts, civilization, language and other studies. According to some accounts, he was assisted by his two sons or brothers - depending what version of the myth you hear - Imaymana Viracocha and Tocapo Viracocha. However, they were not always welcome - some people went as far as to stone Viracocha.

For example, on his way to Cuzco, he encountered people who lived in the province of Cacha. He awakened the Canas people there who emerged from the depths of the Earth but did not recognize the Creator God. They attacked him. But after Viracocha made fire rain from a nearby mountain, they flung themselves at his feet, and Viracocha forgave them.

He then founded the great city of Cuzco, awakening people known as the Orejones - they are said to have been wearing huge golden discs in their earlobes - and they consequently became the rulers of Cuzco.

Eventually, Viracocha made it all the way to Manta, Ecuador and then crossed the Pacific waters, meeting the other *viracochas* along the way. He headed into the West, promising to return one day. Before he left, he told men to beware of 'false men' who would claim that they were *viracochas*.

What can the creation myth tell us about the Incas?

Although little historical evidence exists to confirm the credibility of any part of the Inca creation myth, it is nonetheless important to note as it gives an insight into the mind of an Inca and how their society functioned. For example, the various places from which the Inca emerged - such as waterfalls, springs, and caves - were regarded as sacred, and worshipped by the Incas. They called these sites *huacas,* and believed that a semi-divine spirit inhabited them, often erecting shrines there.

They built special shrines in the places believed to have been visited by Viracocha. For example, where he sent fire to rain over the Canas people, the Inca built a shrine. They also built a bench made of solid gold to hold a statue that Viracocha was believed to have erected at Urcos when he journeyed there. This is also significant because Francisco Pizarro who led the Spanish inquisition later claimed the bench as part of his share of the conquest.

The creation myth also sheds important insight into how the Incas treated other cultures. Although the Incas later built a massive empire that had roughly 10 million subjects, ruled by only 100,000 Incas, they did not impose their religion and statutes over the cultures they conquered. Instead, they incorporated the specific beliefs of each culture into the fabric of their own culture. This was mostly to do with Viracocha's message that tribes had their distinct characteristics that he had created for a purpose, and should therefore all live in harmony. This is very different to the Spanish conquistadors who later tried to impose Christianity upon their conquered subjects.

Chapter 3 – The Founding of the Great City of Cuzco

The city of Cuzco, located in ancient Peru, was one of the most important cities for the Incas. The Incas called it 'The navel of the Universe' and the city flourished between c. 1400 and 1534 AD. During its peak years, Cuzco had as many as 150,000 inhabitants. It was a spectacular city, rich with wondrous buildings and temples, dedicated to their gods.

But how did the Incas arrive at Cuzco?

The Incas epic journey to Cuzco

At the time of the Spanish invasion, the Incas believed that they had only had 13 generations of rulers. They believed their original ancestors were created by the god Viracocha from the sun god Inti. This is where the name 'Inca' comes from - they considered themselves to be 'children of the Sun.' Their ruler, in turn, was the Sun god Inti's embodiment on Earth.

The very first Inca ruler and human, according to their mythology, was Manco Capac. Although he founded the city of Cuzco, he was not originally from there. Following the orders from Viracocha, he journeyed to Cuzco with his *sister and wife* Mama Ocllo, accompanied by three other couples who were also siblings.

One version of the myth tells that the four original couples emerged from a sacred cave. Instructed by Viracocha, they journeyed north for about 30km. Not all of them made it there, though.

One of the siblings turned out to have a spiteful and mean character, and so the others tricked him to return to the cave and then rolled a large boulder in front of him, so he remained forever trapped. Another brother was turned into a stone pillar along the way, and yet another was transformed into a pillar at Cuzco.

When the Incas arrived at Cuzco, they discovered it was inhabited by a tribe called Chanca. Nonetheless, Viracocha gave them a sign in a giant rainbow across the sky, to indicate this truly was their promised land. Aided by his promise, and with the help of some stone warriors, the original Incas defeated them. Upon victory, Manco Capac threw a golden rod at the ground and founded the city of Cuzco, consequently becoming the first Inca ruler.

These are the mythical origins of the Inca civilization - but is there any truth in this story?

What archaeology can tell us

Archaeological evidence found in the valley of Cuzco shows that the first settlements were established as early as 4500 BC. The valley was inhabited by hunter-gatherers, who lived in small communities.

However, it wasn't until 500 BC the population settled and made Chanapata their primary dwelling place. Although archaeological digs in the area have produced some evidence of decorated pottery, no evidence has been found from this period to suggest the existence of large buildings, art or metalwork.

At about 1000 AD, these small communities occupied an area of about 60km. The largest towns at the time housed a few thousand people. The central point for these communities was Cuzco. This period is known as Killke or the pre-imperial Inca era. Archaeological evidence shows at around 1200 AD this area was relatively peaceful, however there were some minor conflicts among the communities.

As the years went on, Cuzco became more important to the Incas. From 1200 CE onward the great city began to take shape. Led by their leaders, the Incas began a determined unification of the communities late in the 14th century. According to historical accounts, the Incas did rage war against the Chanca people and defeated them in 1438 AD. This was when Cuzco became the capital of the Inca empire that continued to expand in all directions.

Eventually, it stretched across the Andes, as the Inca conquered many other cultures in their quest for greatness, becoming the largest empire in the Americas and the largest empire in the entire world at that time. Cuzco was the religious and administrative centre of this vast empire, where all the power and wealth derived from taxes was consolidated.

The wealth was evident in Cuzco - each Inca ruler left a grand legacy behind them, complete with their unique palace and a walled residential complex – as well as spectacular temples dedicated to their gods. The city was greatly expanded in the mid-15th century, during the Inca ruler Pachacuti Inca Yupanqui's reign.

Why was Cuzco so important?

With such a vast empire, any city could have become the administrative centre for the Incas. The Incas chose Cuzco. Mythology aside, why was this city so advantageous to them as to be selected as their capital?

Geographically, the city is located on an ancient glacier lake bed (hence the name 'dried-up lake bed'). It is situated in a conveniently and politically advantageous central point between many natural routes, each leading to a different region within the empire.

Several rivers meet in Cuzco, too. Namely, the Huatanay, Tellme, and Chinchilla. For the Incas, this was not only advantageous but held a particular significance also - it was a sign of good fortune. They did tamper with nature a little - the Incas canalized and diverted the rivers to create the space they needed for building their great city. However, they held a firm belief that nature could be adapted but must never be abused.

The valley itself is located at a high altitude, about 3,450m high, surrounded by picturesque mountain peaks. Despite the high altitude, the valley was still a fertile place to grow crops. The hills provided excellent pasture for the domesticated animals.

Thanks to its naturally advantageous location and the Incas creation myth, Cuzco was regarded as a sacred site. Later as the Inca empire expanded, their subjects were made to send tributes to Cuzco in the form of gold, precious artworks and valuable artefacts, and even people. Some came willingly, others as hostages. For example, expert craftsmen and skilled artists were ordered to relocate to Cuzco. Other hostages became sacrificial victims.

To boost the notion of their great city being 'the navel of the Universe,' the Incas improved the natural roads and passages by building paved roads and 41 sacred sight lines. They also had their version of propaganda - miniature models of Cuzco were circulated around their vast empire to show off the wealth and size of their capital.

And yet, the city was sacked by the Spanish conquistadors in the mid-16th century, with the last Inca ruler being executed in 1533. What could have led to such a rapid downfall?

Chapter 4 - The First Dynasty of Inca Rulers and Their Greatest Deeds

The Inca had a special name for their rulers. They called them 'Sapa Inca' or 'Inca Qhapaq.' Translated, these terms mean 'the only Inca' or 'mighty Inca.' They also used the name 'Apu' which means 'divinity.' The Inca saw their rulers as direct descendants of the god of Sun, known as Inti.

Manco Cápac (c. 1200 to 1230 AD)

This lineage began with their very first ruler Manco Cápac. He was the one who, according to myths, journeyed all the way to Cuzco valley and founded the great Inca city. The Inca rulers who succeeded him wore *mascapaycha*, a ceremonial band of red wool on their foreheads, with fringed tassels of gold thread. This headware had a symbolic meaning - whoever was wearing it held the most power in all the Inca kingdom.

The Inca rulers can be divided into two dynasties.

The Húrin dynasty

There is little historical evidence regarding the rulers from the first of these two dynasties - except their rule did not extend much further than the Kingdom of Cuzco. Manco Cápac was succeeded by his son.

Sinchi Roca (c. 1230 – 1260 AD)

According to one version of the Inca foundation myths, it was Sinchi Roca, the son of Manco Cápac, who led his entire family to the valley of Cuzco. His father named him as the successor to his throne, instructing him to care for his children and their descendants.

He is believed to have married Mama Cura, who came from the lineage of Sanu and together they had a son Sapaca. She may have been his sister which would have been a tradition at the time.

Sinchi Roca was a peaceful man and did not get involved in military exploits. Except when a situation called for prompt action, as in the case of Teuotihi. He was a diplomat the Incas had sent to a neighbouring kingdom to deliver a critical message. Ignoring the peaceful gesture, their neighbours killed Teuotihi and sent his head to Cuzco in reply. Thus, a war ensued, culminating in the Battle of Mauedipi where the Incas won a decisive victory.

Legends say the Inca kingdom expanded at this point, but no supportive archaeological evidence has been found thus far in favour of this claim. It is believed that no lands were added to the Inca kingdom during the reign of Sinchi Roca.

Instead, most of his efforts were focused on improving the land and the lives of people in Cuzco. According to the accounts of the chronicler Pedro Cieza de Leóne, Sinchi Roca improved the fertility of the land in the valley by building terraces and importing large quantities of soil. While his father and mother were still alive, Sinchi Roca also erected the House of the Sun.

An unusual part of his legacy is that his name *sinchi* came to signify a local ruler while his father's name *cápac* became a title that was given to warlords.

When it was time to hand over the throne to his successor, Sinchi Roca did something unusual. As opposed to his father, he named his youngest, rather than eldest son Lloque Yupanqui as the next ruler.

Lloque Yupanqui (c. 1260 – 1290 AD)

Just like his father Lloque Yupanqui was not interested in wars, so no additional lands were added to the Inca kingdom. He focused on making the kingdom better from within. During his reign, he succeeded in establishing a public market in Cuzco.

He also built an educational institution, Acllahuasi. Translated, it means 'the house of the chosen ones.' It was a centre for educating women. Later, when the Inca kingdom had grown to the size of an Empire, Acllahuasi gathered young women from all corners of the land.

Mayta Cápac (c. 1290 – 1320)

Until Mayta Cápac's reign, there was no real need to initially expand the Kingdom of Cuzco.

There were numerous reasons for expanding the Inca empire, but one possible explanation is drought. Some of the farmlands in the Cuzco valley were either abandoned or simply less productive than previously. To maintain their standard of living, the Incas had no choice but to go out and conquer new lands that would provide them with the necessary resources.

Mayta Cápac was the right man for the job. As opposed to his more peaceful predecessors, he was described as an aggressive youth, inclined towards fighting from a young age. According to the chroniclers Pedro de Cieza de León and Pedro Sarmiento de Gamboa, some of the war conflicts for the Incas during Mayta Cápac's reign started as a quarrel between him and some boys from a neighbouring group. It is not clear who started it first, but one of the parties was guilty of stealing some water from the other. The disagreement escalated into a war that Mayta Cápac, now a ruler, won. Following their success, the Inca soldiers looted homes, captured lands and imposed a tribute on their enemies.

Mayta Cápac was very young when he assumed the throne. Therefore his father's brother was named as the regent until he came of age.

With his wife Mama Cuca, Mayta Cápac had many children, including his successor Tarco Huamán. He was to become his rightful heir, but Tarco Huamán's reign was short. After a few short years, his cousin Cápac Yupanqui instigated a coup in his palace and took the throne by force.

Cápac Yupanqui (c. 1320 – 1350 AD)

Cápac Yupanqui was the last ruler of the Húrin dynasty. He was known as the 'splendid accountant Inca.' His elder brother Cunti Mayta earned himself an important title, too - he became the high priest of the Inca kingdom.

Cápac Yupanqui is remembered as a man who imposed a Draconian administration upon the Inca kingdom. His first act was to proclaim a death sentence upon the nine surviving siblings of Tarco Huamán, to ensure that no one could contest with his claim for power. He also expelled some of the Inca from the city. His claim to power was supported by his lineage to Mayta Cápac, who was his uncle.

According to the chronicler Juan de Betanzos, Cápac Yupanqui was the first Inca ruler to conquer territories outside of the Cuzco valley. The legends surrounding him commemorate him as a fierce warrior. He occupied the region of the *Cunti* in the north and *Colla* in the south.

Following this, another tribe known as *Quechua* asked for his assistance in their war against *Chanca of Andahuayllas*. After successfully defeating them, Cápac Yupanqui expanded his influence further upon the region.

But he was more than just a warlord. According to the chronicler Garcilaso de la Vega, Cápac Yupanqui also made many significant improvements within Cuzco. These included numerous buildings and bridges, new roads and even aqueducts that conveyed water to the inhabitants of the city.

However, things did not end well for Cápac Yupanqui. After conquering the lands of *Cuyo* and *Anca* some 22 km from Cuzco, Cápac Yupanqui felt inconvincible. He managed to make allies of another dominant force, the *Ayarmaca*. Threatened by the growing power of the Inca kingdom, their ruler offered his daughter as a wife.

The Inca rulers could have thousands of wives, and Cápac Yupanqui was no exception. His decision to marry again enraged one of his principal wives Cusi Chimbo. Allying herself with Inca Roca who belonged to an opposing faction and later became a successor to the throne, Cusi Chimbo poisoned her husband.

Chapter 5 - The Second Dynasty of Inca Rulers and Their Greatest Deeds

Cápac Yupanqui was the last Inca ruler from the Hurin dynasty. His rightful heir Quispe Yupanqui was killed in a rebellion between the *hanan* and *hurin* lineages, who elected Inca Roca as their ruler. He became the first ruler of the Hanan dynasty.

Inca Roca (c. 1350 – 1380 AD)

Inca Roca was proclaimed king after the Temple of the Sun was invaded by his supporters. Accounts about Inca Roca's parentage vary but he is believed to have been the son of Cápac Yupanqui with another wife.

Inca Roca was quick to marry his father's wife Cusi Chimbo and just as quickly poisoned her. He left the Temple of the Sun to the High Priest and built himself a palace complex to display his power. The remains of his palace still exist today - the walls of his palace can be seen in the Plaza de Armas in Cuzco.

Using clever diplomacy tactics, Inca Roca succeeded in ending many of the inter-ethnic disputes within the Inca kingdom and started to take on the neighbouring groups. He conquered the *Masca, Pinagua, Quiquijana* and even *Caitomarca* that was located some 30km from Cuzco. However, he ended up losing *Caitomarca* because he did not put any garrisons there. Inca Roca's tribe was a small ethnic group who saw their military exploits as an opportunity to plunder and pillage, rather than the annexation of the territories they conquered.

And then, a misfortune befell Inca Roca. His son Tito Cusi Huallpa whom he'd named as his successor, was taken hostage by the *Ayarmaca* who fought against the Inca and the *Huallacan* (who'd given one of their princesses as a wife to Inca Roca, even though she was promised to one of the *Ayarmaca* rulers). However, the conflict was resolved and peace celebrated among all the ethnic groups before Inca Roca died, and Tito Cusi Huallpa was safely returned to his rightful place as his father's heir.

Yáhuar Huácac (c. 1380 – 1410 AD)

Yáhuar Huácac was the name Tito Cusi Huallpa adapted after he took the throne. It means 'the one who cries bloodied tears' and its symbolism originates in the tale of his capture by the *Ayarmaca.*

Ayarmaca kidnapped Yáhuar Huácac when he was eight. This is because his mother Mama Mikay had initially been promised to one of their leaders before she married Inca Roca. She was a *Huayllaca* woman, and as revenge, the *Ayarmaca* decided to go to war with *Huayllaca*. To end this, *Huayllaca* gave her son Yáhuar Huácac to the *Ayarmaca,* and the group held him captive for many years.

Yáhuar Huácac cried tears that looked like real blood over his sad fate. His abductors were astounded by the miracle and soon became very fond of Yáhuar Huácac because of his charming personality.

He assumed the throne after his escape from captivity at 19, aided by one of his captor's mistresses Chimpu Orma. According to some sources, Yáhuar Huácac conquered Pillauya, Choyca, Yuco, Chillincay, Taocamarca, and Cavinas, adding them to the Inca kingdom.

However, Yáhuar Huácac's troubles didn't end there. Both he and the son he'd named as his successor was murdered. The elders were left to choose the next ruler.

Viracocha Inca (c. 1410 – 1438 AD)

Viracocha Inca assumed the name of the creator god after allegedly seeing visions of the creator god in Urcos. He went further still. After he took the throne, he was quick to declare he'll "conquer half of the world." He was described as warlike yet valiant, and his two captains Apu Mayta and Vicaquirau succeeded in subduing the lands within eight leagues of Cuzco. What's more, he was considered to be the first Inca ruler who ruled over the territories he conquered, as opposed to his predecessors who had merely raided or looted the territories without much further action.

Despite this, Viracocha Inca was threatened by the Chankas who had a similar force to the Incas. He fled Cuzco after his advisors told him to do so during a particularly fierce Chanka attack. According to the chronicler Juan de Betanzos, the Chankas justified the invasion by stating that they were offended by the Inca ruler taking on the name of the Creator god. He took some of his sons with him, but one of them rebelled against his father's decision. Cusi Inca Yupanqui said that he would not abandon Cuzco and the House of the Sun during this crisis. The night before the battle, he apparently had a vision from the gods, showing that during tomorrow's battle even the stones would raise up to lead the Incas into victory. Together with his brother Inca Rocca and six other chiefs, Cusi Inca Yupanqui defeated the Chankas.

But instead of being pleased with his son, Viracocha Inca was furious and refused to accept the spoils. (In the Inca tradition, this was usually done by the king walking on the heads of the defeated enemies.) He was so furious, in fact, he named another son as his successor and ordered for someone to kill Cusi Inca Yupanqui.

But his son survived and changed his name to Pachacuti or 'the turner of the earth.' He spent 20 years rebuilding Cuzco to be in the shape of a Puma. Pachacuti did pay a visit to his father and even invited him to come to Cuzco. When he did, Pachacuti greeted him with insults. He told him he had acted as a cowardly woman and had no right to rule. Viracocha abdicated his throne in favour of Pachacuti, and spent the rest of his days in an estate built especially for him.

Pachacuti (c. 1438 - 1471 AD)

Now we finally come to the Inca Empire or *Tawantinsuyu* (meaning 'four parts together') that was established by Pachacuti.

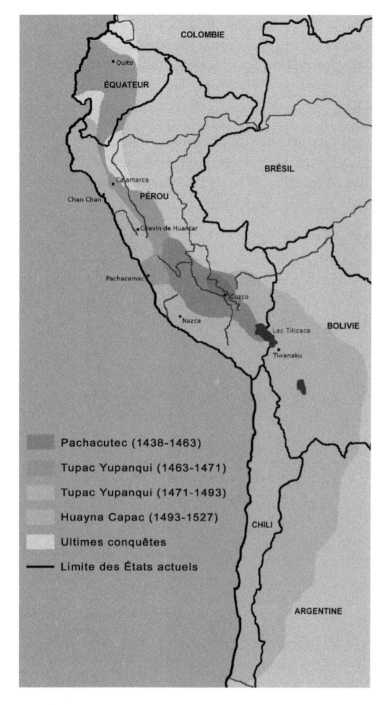

Map of the Inca Empire

Aside from being known as the 'turner of the earth,' Pachacuti was also known as 'the earth shaker' or 'he who overturns space and time.' Although the Inca rulers before him had their fair share of conquests, Pachacuti was the one who began an era of conquest. Within the next three generations, the Inca Empire would spread from the valley of Cuzco to almost all western South America. This included many ethnic groups and states. Thanks to his success, numerous epic stories have been created and told for centuries about Pachacuti's success. He's recognized by many as the true 'son of the Sun.' He not only conquered many lands but also added Inca garrisons in those lands.

However, his story has a dark side, too. Inca rulers always had to stay on their guard to repel any claims to the throne. This may be why Pachacuti murdered his two brothers Ccapac Yupanqui and Huayana Yupanqui, as well as his sons Tilca Yupanqui and Auqui Yupanqui.

Chapter 6 – The Rise of the Inca Empire: A Cosmological Event?

It took only 90 years for the Incan Empire to grow from 100,000 inhabitants to a force of 10 million. What was the key to its success? And why did this vast army practically surrender to the comparatively tiny Spanish force?

Dr. William Sullivan, a scholar of Native American cultures, has dedicated his entire life to unlocking the secret to the abrupt fall of the Incan Empire. In an extraordinary study presented in his book *The Secret of the Incas: Myth, Astronomy, and the War Against Time* and Timeline's Ancient Civilization Documentary *The Secrets of the Incas,* Dr Sullivan argues that the rise and the fall of the Incan Empire could be explained by the events that took place in their skies.

While they did not have a sophisticated system for writing, the Incas encrypted the biggest events from their history in the oral myths that were passed on from generation to generation, and are still being told in Peru today. Dr. Sullivan's study of these myths as a way to decipher the prophecies that the Incas perceived in the night sky, brings this culture closer to home, giving it a more human touch than mere historical accounts.

The importance of Cosmology in farming practices

To a modern mind, it is perhaps difficult to grasp the full significance that the alignment of planets and stars had on the mind of the Incas. We rarely venture outside to look at the stars, and when we do, often we can't see fully see them because of the pollution. Gazing at the night sky is indeed one way to put things into perspective, to transcend the day-to-day nuisances that trouble us, and to feel as though we are part of something much bigger than ourselves.

In stark contrast to us, the Incas lived and breathed nature and astronomy. They had incredibly sophisticated ideas of the night sky, considering the tools they had at their disposal. Although they did not linearly measure time as we do today, the Inca farmers relied on their observations in nature when it came to planning when to plant and harvest their crop.

For example, they observed the movement of the constellations to predict climate changes. Namely, the onset of a phenomenon we call El Niño - a band of warm ocean water that develops in the central and east-central equatorial Pacific at irregular intervals (every two to seven years). It causes global climate shifts, such as intense storms in some places and droughts in others.

The Incas knew they couldn't prevent it from happening, but they could prepare for it. To prepare themselves for El Niño and protect their crop, the Inca developed a way of predicting the onset of the phenomena so they could start their agricultural year earlier, raising their irrigation systems.

They used a method that is still in use by traditional potato farmers in Peru today. In June, six months before Christmas when the pool of warm water caused by El Niño is at its warmest in the Pacific waters near South America, they watch the night sky. If the star cluster known as Pleiades or Seven Sisters is clear, the farmers plant their crop as usual.

However, if it is obscured by atmospheric clouds, the farmers know that drought is likely to occur. To ensure that their crop survive, they adjust the planting dates of potatoes, their most important crop.

The Milky Way and its constellations

Dr. Sullivan's research suggests the Incas did not only rely on the stars to inform them of changing weather patterns - Cosmology was at the very heart of the Inca civilization.

The Incas saw everything that happened on Earth as an expression of what was happening in the sky above them. They had a corresponding practical action to everything that took place in the sky - on Earth; they worked hard to grind their crops with a millstone. Similarly, the gods ground the fate of the Incas in the sky.

Some of their creation stories also state that after their creator god Viracocha shaped the original few men and women out of clay, he asked them to emerge from 12 different places. So, they became 12 tribes, each representing a different constellation. Inca was one of these tribes. They were all to exist in perfect harmony and work with each other just like the 12 constellations worked in harmony in the night sky.

The constellations in their understanding of the Universe had different names to what we know of them today. These are the names the Inca gave to the central "dark cloud" constellations of the Milky Way (which they believed was the causeway linking men to gods) and their corresponding myth.

Mach'acuay - the Serpent

Mythology: For the Inca, snakes were mythological creatures. They even believed rainbows to be a type of snake.

Location: The *Mach'acuay* constellation is located on the Milky Way between the Southern Cross and Canis Major.

Time of appearance: For the Incas, the Serpent constellation emerges in August with its head-first and starts to set in February.

Interesting fact: Believe it or not, the few snakes that do inhabit the Andean areas become more active during the rainy season which takes place between December and February.

Hanp'atu - the Toad

Mythology: The Toad was an equally important mythological animal to the Incas, just like the Serpent.

Location: *Hanp'atu* can be seen in the night sky, chasing the Serpent away in August; it's a sort of dark cloud set between the Southern Cross and the Serpent's tail.

Time of appearance: This segment of the Milky Way becomes visible in Peru in August, signifying the start of the planting season.

Interesting fact: The toads who inhabit the Andean areas become more active when the rainy season is on, croaking more loudly when their constellation rises in the sky.

Yutu - the Tinamous birds

Mythology: Tinamous are birds that resemble partridges, commonly found in the Andean region. These birds eat small lizards and frogs, echoing the myth that the constellation *Yutu* chases *Hanp'atu* (the Toad) away.

Location: Yutu is the next constellation to emerge - it's a kite-shaped spot.

Time of appearance: *Yutu* emerges in its full glory when the Milky Way becomes visible in the night sky.

Interesting fact: After mating, the Tinamous female bird flees the nest and leaves the male to incubate the eggs - they may come from as many as five different males!

Urcuchillay - the Llama

Mythology: Arguably, *Urcuchillay* was the most important constellation for the Inca. Similarly, llamas were significant to the Inca - they provided food, served as a mode of transport for carrying goods and as sacrifices to the Inca deities.

Location: The constellation rises after the *Yutu,* and consists of llama mother and llama baby.

Time of appearance: *Urcuchillay* rises in November, with the two stars Alpha Beta Centauri serving as its "eyes."

Interesting fact: Llama sacrifices usually took place during critical astronomical events, such as the equinox or solstice.

Atoq - the Fox

Mythology: Andean foxes eat baby vicuñas, close relatives of llamas. But when this happens, the adult vicuñas team up and try to trample the foxes to stop them stealing their babies.

Location: The *Atoq* appears at the foot of the llama as a small black splodge.

Time of appearance: The Sun passes through this constellation in December.

Interesting fact: Andean baby foxes are born in December.

You may have noticed the interesting coincidence between the events on Earth (such as foxes being born when the constellation of Fox rises in the night sky). To the Inca, this was no coincidence, but rather yet another reminder of the interconnectedness of all matter.

According to Gary Urton, Dumbarton Oaks Professor of Pre-Columbian Studies at Harvard University: "The universe of the Quechuas is not composed of a series of discrete phenomena and events, but rather there is a powerful synthetic principle underlying the perception and ordering of objects and events in the physical environment."

What's more interesting is that many of the Inca temples in modern-day Peru resemble these constellations in how they were built. For example, there was a huge building built in the shape of *Yutu*, just beneath where that constellation would rise in the sky. It is still a great mystery as to how the Incas could be so precise and construct these temples so accurately. What is certain, however, is the extent of the Inca devotion to astrology.

Cosmology as a means to predict events on Earth

Now, picture what would have happened if people like the Inca, steeped so deep in cosmology and so reverent of their gods, suddenly discovered there had been a shift in the night sky. For instance, if Yutu could no longer be seen on the Milky Way, or if Urcuchillay did not rise in its usual place. For the Inca, this could mean only one thing - that the causeway between men and gods had been severed, and a major change was coming their way - an unwelcome change.

Dr. Williams had used several techniques for comparing various myths that he's come across during his travels to the Peruvian mountains with the way the constellations would have looked hundreds of years ago when the ancient Inca looked up at the night sky. He believes astrological phenomena coincided with the onset of an 800-year-long civil war in the Andean area back in 650 AD.

He also believes the Inca observed an even more significant astrological phenomena in 1442 AD, roughly 100 years before the arrival of the Spanish conquistadors. Whereas the previous sighting prophesied the onset of a long war, this next sighting foretold the end of the Incas, a break with the gods and their ancestors.

The Incas believed in the saying: "As above, so below." So, when they saw the shift in the stars, they were likely to mourn and eventually accept their fate as a destitute civilization.

Pachacuti, the Inca ruler who reversed the equation

However, one Inca ruler chose life instead. He thought of a radical idea that no one had thought of before. If the events that took place on Earth resembled those of the Heavens, then the reverse must also be true.

Spurred on by another astrological phenomenon (a unique conjecture between the planets Saturn and Jupiter that, according to Dr. Williams, could have been interpreted as the creator god Viracocha handing power to Pachacuti), he began an era of conquest. Within three generations the Inca dominion would expand massively, covering almost the entire Western region of South America.

But what could have been at the heart of his success? Dr. Williams believes that Pachacuti had a unique mission - to have a chance at reversing the prophecy, he would need to work hard to reunite the 12 original tribes of the creation myth who had suffered a great deal in the 800-year-long civil war. This, he believes, would have proved to the gods that they deserved a second chance.

The role of children sacrifice

Just like it's difficult for our modern minds to grasp the effect of the constellations on the Ancient Inca, it is even more difficult to understand how such a sophisticated culture could have exercised the gruesome rite of child sacrifice. Such a horrid act cannot be justified - we can only attempt to understand the motivations behind it, lest we run the risk of reducing the Inca to nothing more but savage beasts.

The Inca believed that, just like the 12 tribes had come from the stars, so did every human. And after they died, each one of them would return to their heavenly home once again. Dr. Williams believes the sincerity of their mission to overcome the prophecy could only be measured by the extent of that which they were willing to sacrifice. What higher price could a nation pay than the sacrifice of its offspring?

The Inca believed the children would act as messengers who would deliver their plea to the gods when they returned to their celestial bodies. This is why they picked two children from each tribe so that each heavenly deity would be spoken to.

How did the Incas expand their Empire?

The Incas, especially their emperor Pachacuti, had a strong desire or motivation for expanding their Empire to the extent that they did - if we take Dr. William Sullivan's view, then they did this in an effort to reverse the prophecy of their empire that the Incas had seen in their celestial bodies. But how did they practically win over such a vast area of land, people and tribes?

Diplomacy

Although they were no stranger to warfare, the Incas always began their conquests by diplomatic means. They negotiated with the local rulers and bribed them by promising good posts and rich rewards, if they cooperated. Their early imperial success owes much to building strong alliances, conscripting defeated enemies into their own army and confronting small target societies and tribes with an overwhelming force - without actually fighting them. Once they achieved their desired effect of overwhelming a target society, the Inca messengers offered them favorable terms of surrender: elites received gifts and could keep their status in society while communities could keep

---

many of their resources and customs. Thus, many of the societies that the Incas targeted were simultaneously charmed and frightened into surrender.

Fortifications

As the years went by, the Incas shifted their attention from small-scale victories to imperial domination. The larger the empire grew, the more resources they needed to rage a war. To save their resources, the Incas built a network of internal garrisons, frontier fonts and systems of roads, with storage depots and support facilities for the army. The Incas also resettled restive people and fortified hot spots, in particular.

Still, there were few fortified strongholds, except in the hostile Northern Ecuador and the southeastern frontier. There's an especially high concentration of Inca forts near Quito, especially at Pambamarca. The purpose of these was to deter raids or cut them off from behind, rather than deflect or defeat potential attacks from outside enemy forces.

Strategy and logistics

Even when it came to fighting a battle, the Incas were master planners and owed much of their success to excellent strategy and logistics, rather than training of their soldiers, battle tactics or technology. The Incas were at their best preparing for a battle, and, as the Inca empire grew, the emperor himself was in charge of strategic planning. The different ethnic groups that made up the Inca army were led by their own lords.

As they travelled to the designated battlefield, the vast armies camped in tents, supported by provincial centres along the main roads that could assist the soldiers and provide resources for them. An array of storehouses supported the soldiers with food, arms, clothing, and other items. The only transport was llama caravans - otherwise the soldiers and their kin travelled on foot.

Battle tactics

The actual battles were either great melees on open terrain or assaults on fortified strongholds. The Incas also employed feigned withdrawals paired with pincer counterattacks and flanking maneuvers. The victories were grandly celebrated, and the Inca emperor usually tread on their enemy's head in the Golden Enclosure or the main plaza in Cuzco. Others made drinking cups out of the heads of their enemies, or flayed the skin of their enemies and used them to make drums that were played during ceremonial events in Cuzco. Soldiers who'd been particularly courageous and displayed valour were richly rewarded - however, the nobles received greater gifts than the commoners, in accordance to the class structure in the Inca society.

Chapter 7 – Social Order in the Inca Society

The Inca society was built around several complex social rites and rituals, and no one was exempt from carrying these out. That included the nobles and the ruler.

How the Inca state was governed

The Incas called their large empire by the name of *Tawantinsuyu*. Translated from their language Quechua, it means 'The Four Parts Together.' These four parts were called the *Suyu*, and each one was governed by *Apu* who was a great lord. These *suyus* were split into two sectors - the upper sector and the lower sector, in line with the Inca notion of duality.

The upper sector:

- *Chinchaysuyu*
  This area occupied most of highland Peru and Ecuador in the north, as well as the coastal areas. This was the most prestigious part and the most populous one.

- *Antisuyu*
  Spreading northeast, this area contained the eastern jungles and the slopes of the Andean mountains.

The lower sector:

- *Kollasuyu*
  This was the largest yet least densely populated part of the empire, spreading across the south-east. This area included southeastern Peru, highland Bolivia and the northern part of Chile, as well as some of the northwest Argentina. This region was named after the Coya ethnic group who lived on the shores of Lake Titicaca.

- *Cuntisuyu*

  This was the smallest region of the empire, occupying the southwest area of the empire, spreading from Cuzco to the southern coast of Peru.

These four quarters of the empire were mirrored in the capital city of Cuzco in the way it was constructed.

The role of social norms in keeping the empire together

To keep such a vast and varied empire together, a competent military force was insufficient. A strict governing structure was also required. This meant every member of the society had to comply with strict social norms and religious rite.

When discussing the social obligations and duties of the various people and casts that made up the Inca society, we once again come up against the unreliability of certain popular historical sources. According to the chronicler Garcilaso de la Vega - an omnipotent emperor governed over a vast and complicated bureaucratic system that included local rulers and governing bodies. However, de la Vega was interested in presenting his ancestors as benevolent monarchs. The opinions that most of the Spanish chroniclers collected were those of the aristocracy, meaning that they were skewed in the favour of the ruling class and peppered with propaganda.

Although some societies that the Inca incorporated into their empire did eventually adapt their customs, many did not and simply carried on with their own religious and social rites whenever they could. They paid their taxes diligently, however the Inca rule went skin-deep and the locals were never fully converted to the Inca belief and social system. Since there were only about 100.000 Inca that ruled over an empire of almost ten million, most of the locals never actually saw a real Inca in their life, and there were hundreds of these smaller individual societies within the Inca empire.

However, there were rules that everyone obeyed, and the king and his wife were no exception to these.

The king and queen

Following the death of a ruler, his inheritance was split into two parts - the most able son inherited the ruling power while his kinship inherited all the king's properties.

The King was an absolute monarch, the divine being of god's representation on Earth. He was the military leader, the head of all the different social groups and the political leader, as well as provided sacred leadership. At least that's the idea that was perpetuated across the Inca empire.

The reality was quite different - the King was constantly torn between pleasing the various aristocratic groups that existed, to make sure that he was recognised as the legitimate successor to a deceased monarch and remained in power until the day he died.

The rulers were advised, counselled and even assassinated by their relatives. Thus, only the king's ideal was omnipotent - in practice, they had to manoeuvre among the different interests and needs of their relatives, lest they are torn from power.

The king had different 'duties' he had to perform during various stages of his life, and not all kings could carry them out successfully. When a new Inca ruler came to power - although he was considered omnipotent and god's representation on Earth - he still had to prove himself as worthy of the title first. This was usually achieved by military means - the Inca rulers had to establish their supreme power by success in military conflict, and win favour with the aristocracy. Once he'd succeeded to impress them, he was anointed as a deity who was supreme among all the other people who walked upon the Earth. While military valour was important, so was the king's sanctity and generosity. Every four days, the king had a duty of provisioning the population of Cuzco with food from the royal store houses.

During the day, the king conversed with the living as well as the dead, eating and drinking with them, before retiring for the night in his palace. When he was granted his title, he assumed a new name that was given to him.

Ritual pomp and feasting comprised the daily routine of a king - from early morning through to late night, the king had to entertain his guests from both upper and lower parts of Cuzco and watch over the regular feasting in Cuzco's central plaza. His guests had to obey certain norms, too. Anyone who approached the emperor had to show their humility by taking off their shoes and loading their back with a small bundle that was a symbol for a burden to carry. When the ruler received visitors or conducted political affairs, he spoke through a screen via an interpreter.

The king's outfit

The Emperor had just as many elaborate costumes as he had rituals and duties.

- Headband of braided cloth sometimes adorned with feathers. The king's crown was a braided cloth that had a fringe that dangled before the ruler's eyes.

- Large ear spools that marked the king's social status and prestige, and were worn by the aristocrats. The Spanish called 'pig ears.'

- A staff, covered in tiny feathers and three larger feathers that projected from the tip of the staff. Used during ritual processions to represent the ruler's power.

- A golden mace and royal stand made of cloth that was painted until it stood stiff.

The installation and death of a ruler

During such events, all of the participants of the royal families of Cuzco gathered in the central plaza to celebrate. The statues of the sun and other main gods were present, as well as representatives of all the important shrines.

During the installation of an emperor, some 200 children aged 4 to 10 were sacrificed, adorned with golden jewelled items, sea shells and statues. The death of a ruler also saw the ritual of human sacrifice, including children, although the number of exactly how many were executed is unclear. The Incas saw children as the purest human beings that gave them a special sacrificial status, and the ones chosen for sacrifice had to be particularly physically healthy.

The sacrifice of children was a long affair, and it did not take place in the same plaza as the celebrations. Months or sometimes even years before the event, the children were fed with elite diets, consisting of maize and animal proteins. When the day of the sacrifice drew nearer, they were dressed in expensive clothes and adorned with jewels, ready for their sacred pilgrimage to Cuzco, where they met the emperor who held a feast to honour the children.

The priests then took the children on a long and arduous journey to a sacred burial site on a high mountaintop. There, children were given an intoxicating drink that minimized both their pain and resistance. The priests then killed the children by strangulation or a heavy blow to the head. The less fortunate ones were left out in the extreme cold until they lost consciousness and died.

The emperor Pachacuti had a special ceremony carried out after his death per his request. He instructed people to mourn for an entire year and to carry his body to all the important sights and places where he'd won great victories while people cheered on.

2,000 llamas were sacrificed in Cuzco in Pachacuti's memory, along with another thousand llamas that were sacrificed all over the empire. Children, too, formed part of the sacrifice.

The king's principal wife

The coupling of the king and his principal wife was not a simple affair. While the women associated with the king (his wife and his mother) could enjoy privileges, they also had unique duties they had to perform, and they were subject to as much danger as the king himself if he were overthrown. In line with the Inca notion of duality, the king and his principal wife formed a perfect union.

Tupa Inca Yupanki, the second Inca ruler, began the tradition of marrying his sister and being coronated together as a married couple. This was always the sister from the same father, but she may have had a different mother. Although this idea may seem abhorrent to us, it did reduce bloodshed and the number of claims that could be made for the throne during the Inca civilization. The principal wife had her line of duties to perform. She was seen as *coya* (or queen) and as the mother of the nation.

Before she could become a *coya,* the queen had to meet certain standards. She had to have pure Inca blood flowing in her veins. She had to be the king's sister or one of his first cousins. She had some independent power, and she could act as a persuasive political advisor to her husband and his succeeding son. Traditionally, it was the woman's role to promote a selected son as the royal successor. The mother was crucial because the rulers did not belong to a particular kin group but founded their own, closely identified to that of their mother's.

The wife was the liaison between the ruler's relatives and the king. The mother of the king held a influence, and she was just as influential after death as she had been while she was alive. This was done through a medium or an interpreter who spoke on behalf of an image or a mummy of a deceased queen.

But women associated with the king (like his wife or mother) did not only enjoy privileges - they also encountered certain dangers when a change of politics occurred. For example, if a king was overthrown in a coup, he may have been spared but his mother would not. A good example of this was the defeat of Vascar by Arualpa - when he was defeated, Vascar, his wife, and his mother were taken as prisoners, while others associated with the king were pardoned.

What's interesting is that the queen's influence increased when she became a mother to the next ruler, and her power continued even after her death. The king's wife or mother was an important advisory.

The king's other wives

The king had many consorts and princesses of royal blood who were his secondary wives. To illustrate just how many different wives a single ruler could have, the last undisputed Inca ruler Huayna Capac took 2,000 of them on the way to his military conquests in Ecuador. His other 4,000 wives were left behind in Cuzco.

The *panaqa*

The *panaqa* was the most exalted kin group at the time of the Spanish arrival. According to the Inca customs, they inherited all the deceased king's properties. However, they had a price to pay - they had to execute all the rituals surrounding the deceased ruler's mummy and perform elaborate ancestor worship rituals.

At the time of the Spanish arrival in 1532, there were ten *panaqa* or ten noble Inca kin groups, who were distant relatives of the royalty. The kin groups in Cuzco were made up of different ethnic groups who had lived in the region when the founding fathers arrived.

Each *panaqa* kin group was formed of descendants of an Inca ruler. The first five of these *panaqas* formed the lower part of Cuzco, and the latter formed the upper Cuzco. Thus, the descent groups who were related to the first five Inca rulers were less influential than the most recent five.

The *panaqa* could nonetheless influence the decisions about who the next ruler should be. Therefore, the kings and the various kin groups were involved in constant power negotiations. It was good news if the king the *panaqas* selected was successful in their claim, and bad news if he was not. For instance, after his victory and return to Cuzco, Arualpa's forces wiped out all the *panaqa* kin groups who'd formed allegiance and supported Vascar. This means the most recent five *panaqa* kin groups were slain, with only few managing to escape and later making a claim to the Spanish king to restore them back to their resources.

Ancestor worship

The Inca's rigid social structure and the division of roles incorporated the living, as well as the dead. This is because the Incas believed the world was divided between the living, the dead, the gods and the spirits and each had their duties to perform. Ancestors were venerated, and they had their duties to perform. Mummies of aristocrats participated in the day-to-day political decision-making and elaborate rituals.

For example, the mummies were brought out daily into the main square to participate in the affairs of the state. The male and female attendants ate and drank on behalf of the mummies. They also made firewood and burned fires in front of each mummy.

The attendants brought all the food they ate and put them in front of the mummies; they then burned in the fires.

Large images of gold, silver, and clay were also placed in front of these mummies, and chicha was poured out for the mummies to drink.

The real mummies only 'attended' the most important rituals. Where participation was not paramount, effigies of the mummies or 'brother images' were sent in their place. The mummies also visited their living relatives, and they weighed so little that they could be carried from place to place on a man's shoulders.

According to the chronicler Pachacuti Yanki, Vascar who raged war against Arualpa asserted his belonging to a royal kinship by having his mother marry his father's mummy. This served to affirm his belonging to the royal bloodline.

What's most peculiar about these tales is that was involved in decision-making, when the living could not agree. Thus, it was more than just a symbolism that the mummies participated in the political decisions.

The Inca aristocrats were masters at manipulating their history for political gain. For example, one family would tell the tales that only represented their lineage in a good light. There wasn't much weight given to the truth - everyone had their version of history.

The life of a local and military service

From birth to death, the local people had to follow specific social rules and rituals. This included military service. At certain times during the year, when they did not have to harvest their crops, the men from different provinces and ethnic groups were summoned to join the Inca military service as a way of paying their tax. There were no means of transport during the Inca days, so many of the soldiers came on foot, dragging their entire families with them (since the military conquests could last a long time). Many died during battles, and it wasn't unusual to see each soldier bringing with him twice as many followers.

The Inca fights were truly spectacular affairs, but the Incas only resorted to these, if they had not managed to succumb an ethnic group or settlement with gifts and bribes. Although the fights were often bloodied and brutal, each soldier dressed in their best garments. Certain ethnic groups wore their costumes, so it was easier to tell during a battle who was a friend and who was a foe. This gave an eerie sense of beauty to the brutal spectacle.

Chapter 8 – The Different Roles of Women in the Inca Society

The Inca believed in the concept of duality.

They also believed other things in life came in pairs. Just like the Moon was not complete without the Sun, and the tears of the Moon were silver while the sweat of the Sun was gold, so a male was not complete without a female. Although women adapted many different roles in the Inca society, they were highly valued and played their role as much within married life, as within the religious ceremonies and advancing political agendas.

Women from ethnic minorities

Many ethnic groups existed within the Inca Empire, and they had their social norms and structures. Many of these underwent significant changes when they were conquered by the Incas.

For example, Christine Hastorf had researched an ethnic group called Wanka who still exist in the Junín Region of modern central Peru and fought fiercely before they were assimilated into the Inca Empire.

Before the assimilation, their households appeared to have been autonomous, socio-economic units. People ate a diet that consisted largely of potatoes, although there has been evidence found to suggest communities of women did process some maize crops in their diet. Nonetheless, the domestic and roles within the community seemed to have been split equally among men and women - the skeletons found in archaeological digs show they ate a diet of similar items at similar percentages. This complementary view of gender aligns with the Inca ideals of duality that may have existed in the rest of the Andean society.

However, things changed after the conquest. The Incas imposed their government upon the Wanka people. From 1460 to 1532 AD the Wanka consumed a lot more corn and almost no potatoes. The households had less freedom now, and this impacted women.

More of the Wanka men became labourers, drafted into the government's work parties who probably used food, particularly meat, and drink as a reward. The role of women degraded, and they were even excluded from important state rituals.

Married women

There was a clear division between married life for the lower classes and married life for the upper classes - namely, in the number of wives a husband could have. The lower classes tended to have monogamous relationships for the simple fact they were unable to support more than one wife and all her children.

In lower class monogamous marriages, women were somewhat more valued. Even before the Incas arrived, many ethnic groups in the Andean vicinity, held the belief that the roles of men and women were complementary and interdependent. The married couple worked as a team. Women were responsible for cooking, looking after children and weaving while men carried out more physical labour. In fact, women had to pay tribute to the state by means of producing a certain number of textiles.

Men from the upper class valued women less. Their wives often came from the *Acllahuasi* or the house of The Chosen Women.

The Chosen Women

The women who were admitted to the *Acllahuasi* became the most educated women in the entire Inca Empire. How did they get in?

As the name suggests, they were chosen by the government officials. Each year, the most good-looking eight to ten-year-old girls from each town were conscripted to enter the *Acllahuasi* by specially elected officials called *Apu Panaca* or 'Lord of the Sisters'.

To be chosen was particularly good news for women from the lower classes, as it allowed them to move upward in society. But not all of them were so lucky. After spending four years in complete chastity studying in the capital city of Cuzco, the women had different fates.

Though it may have been beautifully presented, the idea of the *Acllahuasi* was to fully remove the women from their homes and duties there, so they could entirely devote themselves to the service of the state - mind, body, and soul.

The Chosen Women were instructed by *mamaconas* or teachers in various trades, such as religious rites, secret knowledge, the preparation of sacred foods and the elaboration of fine fabrics. Since clothes were among the most precious gifts the Inca could give to those they favoured, along with cocoa and beautiful women, all the women in these convents learned how to make textiles. They also learned how to brew an important corn drink called chicha.

While some women learned valuable trades, others were less lucky. The best-looking girls, in fact, were chosen for sacrifice to the gods. Others were assigned to become concubines for the Emperor or wives of other important men the ruler wanted to ally or honour. Others still stayed permanently at the *Acllahuasi*, becoming the next generation of *mamaconas*. The upper-class women usually completed administrative tasks while the lower-class women carried out work that involved more manual labour.

There was one important restriction for all of them - these women had to remain chaste for the rest of their lives. If they were found to be pregnant, the woman and her lover were buried alive, according to the laws and customs. This was rarely a problem though since no man could enter the *Acllahuasi* or speak to one of the virgin priestesses.

Women at work

What were the other typical roles of women in the Inca society? While weaving was a woman's profession, they also worked in weaving shops that were owned and overseen by men.

Some women became prostitutes and lived in houses overseen by a supervisor. Although these women were social outcasts who were not allowed to have any contact with non-prostitutes, their supervisor was paid by the government.

Women also became healers and midwives. Some of them even induced abortions.

Conclusion

Although one could argue that overall women were not as highly valued as men in the Inca society, they did carry out some very important tasks behind the scenes.

Within married life, a woman was an indispensable companion to her husband, at least within the domestic structure of the lower classes. Within upper-class marriages, women played an essential role in advancing politics through diplomatic marriage. And within the broader context of society, women were almost solely responsible for running the textile industry, around which the economy revolved.

Women played a crucial, yet somewhat passive rule in Inca society.

Chapter 9 – Inca Religious Order and Ideology

Tradition, politics, and beliefs all served as ingredients to create a potent mix of Inca ideology that served to help them claim supremacy over other cultures.

Incas believed they shared the Universe with the gods, deities and nature spirits, all who needed to be venerated. Just like the Earth was filled with living creatures and spirits, the sky too was filled with animals and gods.

The official state ideology justified the Inca supremacy. The chief god within the Inca pantheon of deities was the Sun god Inti, and the Inca ruler was considered Inti's son.

The cult of the Sun god Inti

Although many other Andean societies held the Moon in much higher esteem, the Incas venerated the Sun god Inti. By 1532 when the Spanish first contacted the Inca civilization, they noted Inti worship outshone all the other deities combined. The Sun was incredibly important - not only because of the role it played in sustaining nature but also for its symbolic meaning for the Inca civilization.

Because the Incas claimed their ruler was the son of the actual Sun god Inti, their ruler could claim supremacy in the natural order of things. He was the son of the most important celestial body, and therefore the Inca society was superior to others. The Incas believed a reverence for the Inca ruler was reverence for the Universe itself. They thought they, as a nation, were vital to the world's well-being.

There were two primary visions or representations of the Sun god Inti, as accounted for in various chronicles:

- A small figurine of a boy named 'punchao' (or 'day').

  Solar rays projected from his head and he wore large ear spools, a chest ornament, and a royal head band. Serpents and lions projected out from his body. And he had a somewhat more gruesome attribute, too. The vital organs of the deceased rulers were burned to ash and then inserted into his abdomen so that he could bridge the gap between the divine beings and humanity. In 1572 when the last Inca ruler was executed by the Spanish conquistadors, the idol of 'punchao' that had gone missing for a long time somewhere in the jungle, was recovered. However, it was lost again shortly afterward.

- A more traditional solar disk.

  As opposed to the *punchao* figurine, sources disagree as to whether the solar disk was an authentic Inca invention. It may have been a Spanish invention that was passed down to the Incas. Over the years, as the Spanish and Inca traditions blurred, the solar disk may have been presented as an Inca invention.

The High Priest of the Sun or Inti was usually one of the Inca ruler's close relatives. However, there were some exceptions. The ruler Huayna Capac, for example, took on the role of the High Priest for himself to dispose of a potential threat such a person could cause him.

The importance of the cult of the Sun god could also be seen in the types of buildings that were constructed to Inti. The religious complex of Coricancha or the Golden Enclosure within Cuzco contained the Temple of the Sun that the Inca considered to be at the very centre of the world, and one of its most sacred sites.

The cult of the Sun god generated pretty good income for the state. Every province was supposed to dedicate goods and crops to the Sun, and so there were large storehouses, herds, and staff who were all committed to the church's holdings.

Aside from Inti, there were other deities who were highly esteemed in the Inca religion - Viracocha, the Creator God whom we have already discussed and the moon goddess Quilla (or Mother Moon).

Mother Moon

Quilla or Mother Moon was the wife of the Sun god Inti. Echoing the Inca notions of duality and complementary natures of males and females, Quilal enjoyed similar privileges to the Sun god. Silver was her colour, as opposed to Inti's gold. To the Incas, she was particularly important in calculating time and their annual cycles, many of which were based on the lunar cycle. She was also revered as the deity responsible for regulating the female menstrual cycle.

Beautiful tales surround the other deities within the Inca pantheon, so let's take a brief look at some of them.

Apu Illapu

He was the god of rain and important in agriculture. When people needed rain for their crops, they would turn to Apu Illapu for help. They also believed he drew his water from the Milky Way before he poured it down on earth.

Ayar Cachi

Ayar Cachi was among the first couples that feature in the Creation myth, and set on his way towards Cuzco along with the others. However, his temper was so hot the first Inca ruler Manco Capac decided to lock him up in the same cave he'd come from. The cave is situated some 30km from Cuzco, and the locals believe he's the one causing earthquakes in the area, as he attempts to set himself free.

Pachamama

She was the wife of the Creator God Viracocha (also known as Pachacamac). She was worshipped as the earth goddess or earth mother, a tradition that still exists in the tribes who live in the Andean mountains. People there make offerings to Pachamama in the form of cocoa leaves and *chicha* beer. She is usually worshipped during major agricultural events and occasions.

Sach'amama and K'uychi

These two deities form another illustration of the Inca notion of duality and complimentary natures of the male and female roles. Sach'amama was a feminine deity, also known as Mother Tree. She was depicted as a two-headed snake. However, when she passed on to the heavenly realm, she was transformed into a different deity - K'uychi.

K'uychi was the masculine expression of Sach'amama. He was the rainbow god, associated with fertility.

Despite the mostly complimentary and harmonious natures of the deities, there was sometimes competition among them and their worshippers on earth. Human sacrifice was one manifestation of this contest.

The role of human sacrifice

Although the extent of human sacrifices within the Inca civilization never reached the vast numbers of victims the Aztecs executed as part of their religious rites (believed to be as many as 80,000 during especially important events), the Incas did participate in significant numbers of human sacrifice.

A maximum of 2,000 – 3,000 victims could be executed at any one time as part of the human sacrifice tradition, but many of the religious sacrifices involved llamas or special goods rather than humans. Nonetheless, children were usually among the victims.

The archaeologist, Steve Borget made an astonishing discovery in 1996, while digging near the Moche site. There, he found over 70 remains of dismembered sacrificial victims. What's more, he discovered many of them were sacrificed during periods of heavy rainfall - such periods could be dangerous to the Andean cultures, so it makes sense the Incas conducted religious rites and offered sacrifices to appease their gods during this time.

In fact, human sacrifice was usually done to control the nature and change the mind of the god's. During the Inca rulers, Pachacuti's reign who made a stand to reverse the prophecy that predicted the Inca reign was coming to an end, thousands of llamas were sacrificed each year, during the December solstice. Once the llamas had been killed, the high priests put their blood into tiny jars made of clay and distributed these across the Inca Empire.

Children were also sacrificed during Pachacuti's reign. Usually on mountaintops and at major shrines that belonged to each lineage, with the intention, the children would return to the stars to deliver a message to spare the Inca empire from the prophecy that predicted its downfall.

Annual ceremonies in Cuzco

The annual cycle of ceremonies in Cuzco were all shaped according to the heavens. The Incas were very knowledgeable about the celestial bodies and their movements. This was particularly evident when it came to celebrating the Winter and Summer solstice, events that were accurately predicted. Many of the annual celebrations were also centred around the appearance of the New Moon.

There were two calendars in the Inca system that regulated the annual cycles of worship and celebration - a solar calendar that consisted of 365 days and a lunar calendar that consisted of 28.5-day cycles. There is an 11-day disparity between the two calendars over a year.

Nonetheless, the two calendars led to an elaborate cycle of annual festivities.

The *Inti Raymi* or the Sun Festival (the Summer Solstice)

Translated from Quechua, the name means the Sun Celebration. Today, the festival is celebrated on the 24th of June in Cuzco's Fortress of Sacsayhuaman. According to the Spanish chronicler Garcilazo de la Vega, *Inti Raymi* celebration was one of the most important annual celebrations across the entire Inca Empire. The celebrations lasted for nine days in Cuzco's central plaza.

Only the Sapa Inca, the nobility, and the Inca army could participate in these celebrations, along with the effigies of dead rulers and aristocrats. But it wasn't all fun and games. Three days before the celebrations, the participants had to go through a period of purification. They could only eat white maize and a certain herb known as *chucham* during this period.

On June 24th, the Sapa Inca would take his place on a stage in front of the pilgrims and drink a maize-based rink called *chicha de jora*, honouring the Sun god Inti. Dances, shells and musical instruments accompanied the celebrations. It was a colourful affair too - both men and women painted their faces yellow, wearing deer heads and using their antlers as musical instruments. Women would toss an array of red flowers and colourful feathers at the Inca ruler as he returned to his palace.

There was a darker side to the celebrations, too. The chronicler Juan Betanzos accounts that children under ten years of age were brought to Cuzco to be sacrificed. Black llamas suffered a similar fate, being cut open with a ceremonial knife. Their organs were later used to predict the future.

The Queen's Festival (August)

During the month of the Queen's festival, the purification ritual or *citua* was performed. The ceremony took place during the rainy season when people were prone to fall ill, as a way of purifying themselves and their city and guarding against disease.

Cuzco's residents engaged in some bizarre yet seemingly fun activities to open the festival - they struck each other with torches and shook clothing outside their doorways to purify themselves and 'shake out' negativity and malice.

Usually, the principal men involved in these festivities met together each year to decide how the ceremony would be carried out. Lots of activities took place in Cuzco and the surrounding areas.

To begin, the Incas summoned some warriors who were to stand at the entrance of their main temples, as though they were ready to fight. To defend the city against disease, all seemingly 'sketchy types' had to be expelled from its walls. This included all foreigners and people born with some form of physical deformity. Even dogs suffered and were thrown out due to their howling.

The warriors assembled in the city's main square where they were split into four groups of 100 men. Each group marched in a different direction, to extend the ritual of purification across the whole kingdom. They shouted: 'Get out, disease!' and marched several miles beyond the city.

The Inca and the principal people involved in these ceremonies danced all night, followed by bathing themselves, their clothes and weapons in the rivers and lakes that surrounded the city. They believed by doing this, they let the disease flow out and into the sea. People also fasted as a form of purification, and, just like pilgrims take on sacred journeys today, the Andean people visited sacred sites and shrines where they believed their tribe or kin group to have originated.

Eclipses and Movements of Comets

The Andean people were unable to predict Solar and Lunar eclipses, and, as opposed to other Mesoamerican civilizations like the Maya or the Aztecs, the Incas were frightened of these events. When a Solar eclipse occurred, the Incas consulted the oracles. One of the explanations the oracles provided was that the Inca ruler or a great prince was about to die and thus the Sun had gone into mourning. In response, the Incas fasted, sacrificed animals, and even innocent boys and girls, to appease the gods.

When it came to a Lunar eclipse, the Incas usually believed that a puma or a snake was eating the Moon. To correct this natural sequence of events, the Incas would act as loudly as they could. They beat drums and shouted, whipped dogs until they howled, threw weapons and spears at the moon and did everything they possibly could to frighten the beast away.

The Incas also told future by the movement of comets. For example, the last Inca leader Atahualpa predicted his death when he saw a great comet flash across the skies as he was imprisoned by the Spanish conquistadors.

The role of other Andean religions

Naturally, when ruling over such a vast Empire, the Incas encountered other tribal religions and rites. How did they deal with them? They either incorporated the deities (such as Pachamama) into their pantheon of gods or exploited the religious beliefs and traditions of other cultures for their own political gain.

Each local group in the Andes had their own beliefs and rites. Most of the local tribes did have one common religious feature though, and that was ancestor worship.

Most of the Andean societies worshipped their ancestors. They also knew of a special place (a cave or a natural formation) they believed to have been the place of origin for their society.

This was good news for the Incas who used the religious rites of other local societies to their advantage. For example, they held ancestral mummies of other tribes as hostages in Cuzco to force the locals to come and reclaim them, so they could once again pay homage to them. The Incas went as far as to publicly whip these mummies, until the local people they were trying to subjugate finally gave into them.

But when it came to oracles who could foretell the future, things were different. Allegedly, thousands of oracles existed within most of the Andean societies. Some of these oracles were older than the societies themselves, stretching back thousands of years. The Incas incorporated these oracles into their religion, continuing to consult the same oracles as the societies that existed before them. For example, a notable coastal oracle was Pachacamac whom the local communities had been consulting for at least two thousand years.

Chapter 10 – Tour of the Greatest Inca Sights

The environment of the area that used to be the ancient Inca Empire is truly spectacular. If you take a road trip from Lima, the central coast of Peru and travel about 200km East, you would be starting your journey from the desert coast, passing through a mountain range and its snow-topped peaks, and eventually, end up in the Amazonian tropical rain forest. The Inca Empire included 20 of the world's 34 major life zones, and you would pass from one to the next in within an hour of walking.

This naturally affected how the Incas built their homes and used their environment.

How the Incas constructed their homes

With such a vast mountain range covering a considerable portion of their empire, the Incas naturally constructed their homes high up, many miles above the sea level. About two-thirds of the population, in fact, lived some 3,300m above sea level. This also affected the way the locals could overcome the problem of high altitude, the Incas invented terrace farming. They built steps of land for agriculture down the mountainside, and this helped them to create flat lands even in the mountains. They also had a good irrigation system - the Incas could channel the rainwater through each step of the terraced lands. They also constructed aqueducts that helped them carry the water more efficiently to wherever it was needed.

Although this view may come from the Inca propaganda at the time, it is believed no one went hungry in the Inca empire. The common people may have eaten little meat, compared to the nobles, but everyone was well fed.

In fact, the Inca were the first society to grow potatoes, along with many other crops, such as corn and quinoa. These were the three staple crops of the Inca civilization, and the latter helped them to make many different dishes. These include flour, soups, and cereal. The Incas also ate a great variety of other fruit and crop - tomatoes, avocados, peppers, strawberries, peanuts, squash, sweet potatoes, beans, pineapple, bananas, spices. They also favoured coco leaves to make their chocolate drinks. They were no stranger to the sweeter things in life either as they kept honeybees.

According to some sources, the Inca grew so much food it had to be dried and kept in specially constructed storage buildings.

Due to the high altitudes, the climate was colder than on the mainland, and therefore better suited for storing food. So, the Incas put the food outside to freeze and stamped on it until all the water had gone. To finish the drying process, they left it out in the sun for a while.

Most notable Inca sacred sites

Many of the most impressive Inca religious sites are still visited today. Since everything in the Inca empire was tied up with their religious practices, many of these sites have been built according to the Inca sacred geometry.

Macchu Piccu

Macchu Piccu.

On the top of the list for any tourist setting out to discover the Inca legacy is the stunning site of Macchu Piccu. The ruins of their great temples at Macchu Piccu were rediscovered by a Hawaiian historian Hiram in 1911 after many centuries of total secrecy. The locals knew about the ruins that were located above the Urubamba Valley. But since they were completely invisible from below, the locals were cautious of sharing their coordinates. It was self-contained, as the site was surrounded by agricultural terraces and natural springs where the locals could get water.

Ollantaytambo

Ollantaytambo

Many tourists nowadays start the Inca Trail in Ollantaytambo and make their way to Maccu Picchu over several days of walking. Ollantaytambo was the royal estate that belonged to the Inca Emperor Pachacuti. He conquered the region and served as a stronghold of Inca resistance during the Spanish conquest.

Choquequirao

The main structures of Choquequirao by Bryan Dougherty Source: https://www.flickr.com/photos/bdougherty/102000050

Translated, Choquequirao means 'the Cradle of Gold' and indeed, set in its breathtaking valley; it could be considered to be just that! Like many of the Inca sites, Choquequirao is located at 3,085m above sea level. There is a staircase configuration, made of 180 terraces. Choquequirao is much larger than Machu Picchu and built in a remarkably different style. It is less frequented than Machu Picchu too since access can be a problem.

Inca Pisac

Pisac

Translated, Pisac means 'partridge' and this sacred site was indeed built in the shape of a bird, matching their bird constellations. Where now are only ruins, there was once a military citadel, a complex of religious temples and individual houses. This area overlooks the Sacred Valley, and it is believed this site helped defend the southern entrance to the Valley, connecting the Inca Empire with the borders of the surrounding rainforest.

The Temple of the Sun

Old Coricancha. Public domain. Source: Biblioteca del Congreso de Perú, Grabados & Photographs DivisLa división de fotografías)

Coricancha (or the Temple of the Sun) was the crowning jewel of the Incas capital of Cuzco. The city was located in the shape of a Puma, and the Temple was believed to be its tail. It was the holiest of all sights in the Incan mythology. The Temple's construction began sometime in the 1200 AD, using a particular masonry style that was a signature for the Incas.

The Temple was not only well constructed but also located in a point of geographical importance - it was built in the very centre of four main highways that led out to the four districts of the empire. Thus, it symbolised the center stage that religion played within the Inca Empire. It was a grand building, housing over 4,000 priests and the building also functioned as a calendar. According to Drew Reed who writes for The Guardian: "Shadows cast by stones placed on the foothills could be seen from the temple, marking out the solstice and equinoxes observed by the Incan empire."

Much of the temple was destroyed by the Spanish conquistadors, who melted down much of its gold adornments. They built their cathedral on top of this sacred site, maintaining the original stone foundations. An earthquake destroyed the cathedral a few hundred years later, while its Incan foundations remained intact. Today, it is open and frequented by tourists who visit Cuzco every year.

Chapter 11 - From Pachacuti to the Arrival of the Spanish

Túpac Inca Yupanqui (c. 1471–1493 AD)

This Inca ruler was known as the 'noble Inca accountant.' He was the legitimate successor of Pachacuti who left a vast Empire in his hands. Back in 1463, Túpac Inca Yupanqui had proven his valour when his father appointed him to head the Inca army. He succeeded as a ruler too, expanding the Empire by adding lands northward along the Andes through to modern Ecuador. In fact, he became very fond of Quito, a city in Ecuador. Túpac Inca Yupanqui rebuilt it with architects brought in from Cuzco.

And he didn't stop there. He subdued the Collas and conquered a province known as Antis. He also built a large fortress on the plateau above Cuzco that held storehouses of food and clothing. He also imposed new rules and taxes, appointing two new Governor Generals. He was quite the ladies' man too, leaving behind him 90 illegitimate children and only two legitimate sons. The son Ccapac Huari whom he'd named as his successor was killed soon after his death, clearing the way for his son Titu Cusi Hualpa to become the next emperor.

Huayna Capac (c. 1493–1527 AD)

After his coronation, Titu Cusi Hualpa took on the name of Huayna Capac or 'the young mighty one.' He had no legitimate sons with his principal queen and sister Coya Cusirimay. However, his second royal wife Araua Ocllo gave birth to several sons, including the contender for the throne Huáscar, who'd be engaged in a vicious civil war with his half-brother Atahualpa during the arrival of the Spanish.

Huayna Capac continued with the expansion of the Inca Empire, subduing many tribes in present-day Chile and Argentina, and conquering territories as far north as Ecuador and the south of Colombia. For political gains, he married the Quito Queen Paccha Duchicela Shyris XVI to subdue the Kingdom of Quito in modern-day Ecuador into the Inca Empire. Atahualpa was born of this marriage, and would later battle Huáscar for the throne.

Similarly to his predecessor Túpac Inca Yupanqui, Huayna Capac was also very fond of Ecuador. He built cities there, including Atuntaqui, and he rebuilt Quito, making it the second capital of the Inca Empire. He built astonishing astronomical observatories, too, along with many strongholds.

It was during Huayna Capac's reign that the Inca empire reached the height of its size and power. During its peak, it stretched over a vast area, including many parts of modern Bolivia, Peru, Argentina, Chile, Ecuador, and the south-west parts of Colombia.

Huayna Capac is believed to have died of measles or smallpox, the deadly weapon the Spanish conquistadors had unwittingly carried with them into the lands of the Inca.

Huáscar (c. 1527-1532 AD)

Although Huáscar was Huayna Capac's legitimate heir, his favourite was Atahualpa. Each son was granted a separate realm of the Inca Empire. Huáscar received the southern part with the capital of Cuzco while Atahualpa was given the northern part with Quito as the capital. Things carried on peacefully for four or five years, and together the two sons may have even been able to take on the Spanish. But this was not meant to be, because Huáscar decided he wanted the entire kingdom for himself, throwing the empire into the terrors of civil war.

Translated from Quechua, his name means 'golden chain.' It is difficult to say whether Huáscar was named as the successor, or if it were the nobles in Cuzco who pushed his claim forward, but the fact remains he wanted to rule over the entire Inca empire.

The Spanish chronicler Juan de Betanzos portrays Huáscar as a tyrannical ruler who seized the wives of his lords if they only took his fancy and similarly seized many Lands of the Sun, showing disrespect for the Inca religion. However, the account may be biased since Betanzo's wife was most likely on Atahualpa's side.

The civil war that followed saw some 60,000 men fight on each side, eventually gaining a victory for Atahualpa. However, it was short-lived.

Atahualpa (1532 - 1533 AD)

When the Spanish conquistadors met the still victorious Atahualpa, he was described as fairly short, robust man with an ear that had been damaged in a battle.

The Incas had lots of depictions of Atahualpa on wooden panels and some portraits and tapestries. These were sent to Spain and unfortunately have since been lost.

It's much easier to account Atahualpa's life events though. After defeating and imprisoning Huáscar, the new Inca Emperor massacred all the pretenders to the throne and burned many of the nobles in Cuzco, including several mummies who had allegedly sworn allegiance to Huáscar. Some accounts even say he ripped out the hearts of his opposers and forced their supporters to eat them.

Naturally, after such an astounding victory, Atahualpa underestimated the threat the Spanish posed, led by Francisco Pizarro. However, the measly Spanish force of some 168 men and 69 horses eventually defeated Atahualpa's grand army. Atahualpa was captured and used by Pizarro to control the empire. He was eventually executed, spurring many claims to the throne. However, the Inca Empire had already started to disintegrate and would remain in the hands of the Spanish for centuries.

Chapter 12 – The Spanish Conquest

Perhaps the most baffling fact about the history of the Incas is how such a vast empire - the biggest that the Americas had ever seen - could have fallen so easily to the Spanish of just 168 men?

It is true that Atahualpa's armies had been significantly weakened by the civil war. However, Atahualpa and his forces were still much more powerful than the Spanish conquistadors. So what happened?

Before the conquistadors finally met with the Incas, the Spanish conquest had been in motion for some time. It started in 1492 and by 1519 the Aztec empire in modern-day Mexico had been defeated. Many of the Spaniards embarked on their mission with the objective to find a great fortune. However, not everyone did, and so they carried on with their quest for gold until they finally came face-to-face with the Incas. In fact, out of Francisco Pizarro's 168 men, only 30 came fresh from Spain. The rest of them had spent 10 or 20 years in Mexico, aiding the conquest. They wanted to make their mark on the world, gain new riches and lands, and they had years of battle experience which made them a small yet dangerous force for the Incas.

Pizarro's first encounter with the New World was in 1513, when he arrived in Panama, accompanying Vasco Núñez de Balboa. His first encounter with the Inca Empire was in 1524, and he made a second attempt in 1526. A combination of inclement weather, hostility from the natives and a lack of support and provisions led to failure. However, in 1531 Pizarro returned and, to his advantage, some of the Inca royal court, including the ruler Huayna Capac, were impacted by the Spanish diseases. What's more, the chaos caused by these deaths allowed Huáscar to start a war against his half-brother Atahualpa.

So the odds were in Pizarro's favour. By 1531 his force had made its way to Ecuador, where they gained a victory in the province of Coaque. There they waited a few months for reinforcements to arrive. During that time, they battled with the many diseases that were rampant on the Ecuadorian coast. Just like the natives were unequipped to deal with European diseases like smallpox and measles, so were the Spanish unequipped to deal with the native diseases. Among these was a disease described by their chroniclers as 'berrugas.'

Nonetheless, the reinforcements arrived, and Pizarro reassembled his army in 1532. They headed southwards. Along the way, the Inca ruler sent presents and an invitation to the Spaniards to visit the ruler's camp. It may appear like a generous gesture, but for the Incas such an invitation held a specific strategic message. This was how the Incas traditionally issued a threat to an enemy. But since the Spaniards missed this cultural queue, they advanced at a steady pace. Nonetheless, the Inca probably didn't think anything much of the Spaniards. In November 1532, Pizarro's army reached Cajamarca, near where Atahualpa was taking some long, relaxing thermal baths, having just defeated Huáscar.

Pizarro's men took refuge from the rain and hailstorm in the buildings surrounding the main plaza in Cajamarca. He sent his men Hernando Pizarro and de Soto to meet Atahualpa in the nearby thermal baths, and to invite him back to Cajamarca to meet with Pizarro. Atahualpa was not very interested at first, but once he discovered Hernando was related to Francisco Pizarro, he even offered to host a dinner for the troop.

However, they declined out of caution. They could not pass on the offer to have a drink together, and during this friendly ceremony the Spaniards put on a grand display of horsemanship. The horse came too close for comfort to Atahualpa, and his servants immediately rebuffed the horse and the Spaniards. Unfortunately, the gesture was not well-received - because Atahualpa had remained passive, he expected the same of his servants. Their loyalty couldn't save them, and all four of the servants were executed.

Atahualpa agreed to meet with the Spanish forces the next day in Cajamarca's main plaza. Pizarro wasn't sure how to proceed - should he pretend his troops were a friendly envoy from Spain? Should he ask the Inca to swear his allegiance to the King of Spain? Or should he cut the talk short and launch a surprise attack? Together with his men, Pizarro decided to delay the decision and make up his mind as the talks progressed.

Nonetheless, his army was able to utilize the surroundings of Cajamarca and hid in the many buildings and corridors that wound around the main plaza. They were big enough to hide not only the soldiers but even the horsemen. The Spanish also had an advantage because they were able to block the narrow entrance and exit points to the square.

The Battle of Cajamarca

After much anxious waiting, Atahualpa finally entered the open space. It was a truly spectacular sight. At first, Atahualpa's guard and servants assembled themselves, dressed in various flashy colours. They swept the road and removed straws from it, clearing the way for their emperor. Then squadrons in different dresses appeared all dancing and singing. Then soldiers wearing metal plates arrived, and finally the emperor himself - Atahualpa in all his splendour, adorned with plate shoulders of gold, whose litter was carried in by several servants.

The Dominican friar, a representative of the Vatican, conveyed the 'true faith' to Atahualpa. Through an interpreter, he presented the Emperor with a Bible that was supposed to convey the word of God and explained to Atahualpa that from now on he'd need to pay tribute to the Emperor Charles V.

Atahualpa was interested in his gift. He examined the book, he put it to his ear and finally, with great difficulty, opened the cover - only to assume that he'd been tricked because he could not understand the writing. Angered, he threw the book on the floor. This was the perfect opportunity for Pizarro to launch his attack, as the friar shouted the Inca had blasphemed against the word of God.

The Spanish acted fast - cannons were fired, exploding in the midst of the packed rows of the Inca soldiers. Horsemen and soldiers on foot soon followed suit. They slaughtered everyone without mercy in the close vicinity of Atahualpa. Within the space of just two hours, 7,000 Inca soldiers lay dead, and their emperor - captured. This marked the start of the demise of the Inca Empire.

As well as possessing some strategic advantages, battle wits and experience that allowed the Spaniards to quickly capture the Inca ruler, what other advantages did they have? In other words, how did the two armies compare in terms of weapons and military gear?

The Spanish army

The Spanish army was experienced in battle, and well-equipped. In addition to their foot soldiers (infantry), they also had something that the Incas did not - horsemen (cavalry). The horsemen received higher rewards for successful campaigns, so most soldiers who fought on foot aspired to buy a horse and become part of the cavalry.

The horsemen fought primarily with lances (long wooden spears with steel or iron points) and swords. The lances were incredibly effective at slaughtering native foot soldiers when used by a rider on a horse. The swords were roughly three feet long, narrow and double-edged (sharp on both sides). The Spanish city of Toledo had a reputation for being one of the best places in the world for making swords and armour. The steel swords produced in Toledo had a huge advantage over the arms used by the natives - so much so that the Spaniards actually prohibited the natives from having these swords years after the conquest.

The Spanish foot soldiers also used long-range weapons, such as the 'harquebus' or a type of early musket, and a crossbow. Although the harquebus was slow to load and heavy to carry, it was effective in instilling fear into the native soldiers because they suspiciously believed that the Spanish had the power to create thunder. The crossbow was equally cumbersome to carry and use in a battle against quick-footed native soldiers, so these were not much used after the initial phases of the conquest. Nonetheless, the favourite weapon of the foot soldiers was undeniably a fine Toledo sword that allowed the Spaniards to defeat dozens of natives within the space of a few frantic minutes.

The Spaniards had another advantage - their armour. Made of impenetrable steel that the natives had not seen before, their armour made the Spanish almost invulnerable in direct combat. Helmets, heavy breastplates, arm and leg greaves, a metal skirt and a gorget to protect the neck, covered the Spanish soldiers from tip to toe. Thus, the natives only rarely killed a Spanish soldier, clad all over in armour, as they did not have any weapons designed to pierce through steel.

Last but not least, the Spanish army had another weapon that the natives did not have - their motivation to fight for their own survival among a foreign enemy, the chance to carve out a name for themselves in history books, the passion to fight for the glory of God, the Christian cause and their king, and the irresistible opportunity to gain wealth and power in the process.

The Inca army

The Inca army was very different to the Spaniards - both in their motives and their weaponry. For many of them, fighting in a battle for an Inca ruler was not even a choice. The Inca army consisted primarily of conscripts who had to use their own weapons, led by their own lords who owed their service as a duty to their state. An army would usually be mobilized during the agricultural off-season, so the many different tribes that formed the Inca army were first and foremost farmers.

These were usually sound and married males, aged 25 to 50, who were called into the army on a rotating basis. They brought their wives and kin along with them to battle, all moving on foot to reach the battlefield. Single men between 18 and 25 usually bore cargo and messages for those who would later fight in the war. The soldiers were organized by their ethnic group, each wearing colourful, distinctive clothes and carrying distinctive weapons. This made it easier to distinguish a friend from a foe during a battle.

However, the Incas did have their own personal guard, drawn from Cuzco's aristocracy and known as 'big ears' for the large earspools that they wore. The Incas also had dedicated societies to soldiery, known as *Chachapoyas*. The guards were usually well-ordered but other than that, the Inca army contained few military specialists.

For the Incas, a battle was a ritual affair. Along with their armour and weapons, they also carried a range of idols with them into the battlefield, known as *waq'a*. The soldiers who carried arrows, sling stones and javelins for long-range combat usually preceded troops who bore wielded maces, clubs and spears for hand-to-hand combat. The emperor, of course, was carried in a special litter, wielding slings and spears. Nonetheless, the weapons of choice for the Incas were:

- a stone or bronze star mace with a wooden handle;
- a hard, double-edged palmwood club that was shaped like a sword.

As for their armour, the native soldiers wore quilted cloth that was incredibly effective against Andean weapons - so much so that some Spaniards swapped their heavy armour and chose to wear the Inca armour instead to provide lighter protection. The Incas also wore wood or bronze shields and helmets.

Nonetheless, the weapons of the natives were no match to those used by the conquistadors. Some of the natives carried heavy clubs or maces, or stone axes or clubs with spikes on the end. The heavy armour of the Spanish protected well against the blows inflicted by these weapons. The most lethal weapon employed by the natives was a 'macuahuitl'. This was a wooden sword with obsidian shards on either side - nonetheless, it was no match for the Spanish steel armour or Toledo blade, and a Spanish soldier could easily slay a dozen natives while only receiving a few scratches or bruises in return.

The capture of Atahualpa

Mockingly, Pizarro invited the Inca Emperor to have dinner with him in captivity. It soon dawned on Atahualpa what the Spaniards were after - treasure. He offered to fill an entire room, full with treasure - twice over with silver objects and once over with gold. Pizarro liked the idea and agreed to wait things out until the Inca Emperor fulfilled his promise. In fact, this was beneficial to both parties - the Spanish were able to wait for reinforcements and Atahualpa carried on organising court and making plans for his escape. It was a tricky situation for the Spanish as their tiny force in Cajamarca was surrounded by tens of thousands of Inca armies, who were unsure as to how best to free their leader.

Nonetheless, they were able to explore the lands beyond Cajamarca under a royal order. In fact, the Incas even carried three of the Spanish soldiers on litters all the way to the Inca capital of

Cuzco. During this trip, they met with Huáscar, the defeated Inca prince. Naturally, he offered the Spanish to join forces with him and promised to make them rich beyond belief, if they agreed to help his cause. But the Spanish refused, and soon after Atahualpa heard word of this and ordered for Huáscar to be executed.

By April, the Spanish reinforcements had arrived. Equally, Atahualpa had fulfilled his promise and filled an entire room (about 7m wide and 5m tall) with gold and two more rooms with silver. Since they now had a fortune of about $50 million, the Spanish decided the Inca ruler was no longer of any use to them. Pizarro, however, had grown fond of Atahualpa - he'd learned how to play chess, and they dined together frequently. He wasn't sure what to do, as Atahualpa could be useful as a prisoner. Nonetheless, the growing tensions among the Spanish demanded his execution.

A court was conducted, and Atahualpa was convicted of 12 charges, including treason. He was accused of killing his brother and also plotting against Pizarro. He was offered to be burned at the stake or executed by garrote if he became a Christian. Because he needed his body for his own religious beliefs, Atahualpa opted to become a Christian. On July 26, 1533, the last independent Inca ruler was executed by garrote.

After Atahualpa's death

Although Pizarro was somewhat forced into deciding to execute Atahualpa due to the growing discontent among the Spanish forces, not everyone agreed with it. King Charles seemed to have been displeased with Atahualpa's execution since he was a monarch and had to be treated as such. He was called back to Spain to explain himself.

The Incas were confused and divided. Atahualpa's supporters were naturally upset and despaired. But Huáscar's supporters were delighted. The Spanish now needed a 'puppet' to rule on their behalf, and they installed the younger brother of Huáscar and Atahualpa, called Túpac Huallpa. Along the way from Cajamarca to Cuzco, this new ruler died of a disease.

With or without a leader, the Spaniards carried on their journey to Cuzco. There, another Inca prince Manco Inca Yupanqui joined their quest. Together, they marched on Cuzco, a year to the day since their first encounter in Cajamarca.

Three years later, Manco Inca Yupanqui was tired of co-ruling with the Spanish. They had thrown a lot of the nobles out of their homes, they were disrespectful towards the Inca culture, and he wanted to rule independently. So he escaped Cuzco, with plans to raise an army and defeat the Spaniards. He succeeded and raised an army between 200,000 and 400,000 men and attacked the Spanish forces in Cuzco. But despite his best efforts - Manco Inca Yupanqui tried to burn the city, then flood it - the Spanish resisted. Soon, the great Inca army began to disintegrate - it had been formed of local farmers who had to return home to attend to their crop. After ten long months of siege, Manco Inca Yupanqui retreated, founding a Neo-Inca state in the remote jungles of Vilcabamba. It would last until the death of the last independent Inca ruler Túpac Amaru in 1572.

Conclusion

The Spanish did not possess any superpowers, nor did they have a massive force behind them. Their success was down to some circumstances that fell in their favour, paired with their military experience and motivation to fight for God and glory.

1. The civil war between Atahualpa and Huáscar weakened the Inca armies and split the Inca empire into two parts - it was not united when the Spanish arrived. Thus, almost half of the Inca population (those on Huáscar's side) saw the Spanish as their saviours and were ready to join them to fight Atahualpa. In addition, since the Inca Empire ruled over many native tribes and cultures, many of the locals hated the Incas and wanted to see them be overthrown and liberated from their oppressors.

2. Atahualpa's recent success made him underestimate the threat that the Spanish posed. Preoccupied with fighting Huáscar, he missed many opportunities to attack the relatively small Spanish force.

3. The Spanish had advantages in the arms they carried and the armour they wore. They also had horsemen - this was absolutely new to the Incas whose armies always moved on foot.

4. The Incas had been weakened by European diseases, such as smallpox and measles.

5. The Andean army was not always happy to be fighting. It was formed of farmers who were unskilled soldiers, compared to the Spaniards. They completed their service as a tax and had to go back to their crops when the agricultural season was up. Therefore they were not fit for a long-term war. The Spanish army, on the other hand, consisted of seasoned warriors, most of whom had spent decades fighting in Mexico and only a fraction of their men were fresh from Spain. And their motive was possibly their biggest asset - the Spanish were fighting for their own wealth, power and glory, the glory of their King and their God.

6. After Atahualpa's death, the Incas did not have a strong leader. Since the Incas had ruled over many native tribes, the population remained fractured.

Chapter 13 - The Aftermath and the Inca Legacy

Once the Inca Empire and the Neo-Inca state had been successfully defeated, a civil war broke out among the Spanish. In 1541, Francisco Pizarro himself was assassinated by his opponent Diego de Almagro II's men. He was later killed, too. The last Spanish civil war ended in 1554. Thus, for the first 20 years of the conquest, there was no order in the Inca Empire. These are remembered as the 'Black years' by the locals, with many of the local ethnic groups having lost 50% of their population.

All this changed when Viceroy Francisco de Toledo came to power in 1570-72. He moved large numbers of the Andean people out of their traditional communities and into new settlements the Spanish could more easily control. Thus, eliminating the independence, the locals had achieved.

The changing history

Soon it dawned on the locals they were far worse off under the Spanish rule than they had been under the rule of the Incas, so they staged a great number of rebellions (20 to 30 within 150 years). The Spanish prevailed. This is likely when the legends of the Incas were born that presented them in a glorious light.

The local Andeans began to talk about the 'good old times,' omitting details of the oppressive nature of the Inca rule. A whole series of myths emerged, surrounding the return of Inkarrí, an Inca Emperor who would free them of their bonds. This myth is still present today.

The Spanish and their interpretation

The Spanish conquistadors had their part to play in the shaping of the Inca history. When it came to the Inca religion, for example, their priests could only use their Christian faith to reference the Inca and the Andean religions. Therefore, they called the Inca temples 'mosques' because they had not seen anything else. Equally, their priests went to great pains to interpret the local Andean religion in a way that it aligned with the Christian theology. For instance, the flood that the Andean locals mentioned in their myths was interpreted as the Biblical flood.

Only 10 to 15 years after the conquest did the Spanish priests begin to inquire more thoroughly about the local Andean and Inca religions. However, this served the purpose of stamping out their different world views and religious rites, rather than genuinely trying to understand the significance of these rites in the Inca society. By the time their interest became genuine, the Incas had learned to celebrate their rites in secrecy and no longer shared this knowledge with the Spaniards.

The Inca Legacy Today

Remarkably, even all these years after the Spanish conquest, the native Andean people continue to observe many ancient rites and rituals. For example, the people of Cuzco reinstate the June Summer Solstice festival each year with a great ceremony.

The cycles and myths of Inkarrí continue to this day, as the local Andean population, especially among the communities in the Peruvian highlands, who still follow the traditional lifestyle and yearn for the 'good old days.' These people observe the cycles of nature, as their forefathers did before them, and they have a reverence for the sky and the earth, as expressed in their annual practices and ceremonies.

During the 1980s, the Peruvian national currency was called Inti (after the Inca sun god), and today's currency is called Sol, the Spanish name for 'sun.'

The Peruvian election in 2000 is an excellent example of the Inca ideologies that remain potent among the local communities even today. The Inca population raged a series of protests surrounding the presidential election in Peru in 2000. A huge rally was staged in Lima surrounding the political process, and the name given to the rally was 'The March of the Four Parts.' One could just as easily call it 'The March of the Inca Empire.'

Conclusion

Even after so many hundreds of years have passed since the last Inca ruler died, the ancient Inca traditions remain alive today. The local farmers in the Peruvian highlands are still very much connected to the earth and the movements of the sky, which they used to predict the outcome of their crops. That knowledge is perhaps one of the most beautiful aspects of Inca legacy today.

Just as the traditions remain true, so does the yearning to be free people. Any debate about the negative aspects of modern day politics in the modern Peru stirs within the locals strong feelings of once being part of the greatest empire the Americas ever saw.

However, much of this nostalgia may be tainted from the truth of the events. As much as the Inca Empire has been portrayed as a wonderful utopia in many historical accounts, where life was good, this version of the truth likely emerged after the locals felt the price of the Spanish conquest. The Inca Empire was far more than just a stereotype of a perfect kingdom. The story of the Inca Empire is one of 'greys' - ever-shifting perceptions and loyalties, on the backdrop of rigid social norms and customs. It is a history filled with dynastic wars among relatively short periods of peace that eventually served to lead to its demise. To know what a local Inca felt during any one of these periods, or what he thought of his empire, remains a mystery that, even with so much evidence presented, we can guess at best.

Help Requested

If you enjoyed this book, then it would be really appreciated it if you would post a short review for the book on Amazon.

Thanks for your support!

Endnotes

Introduction:

- Cartwright, Mark. *Inca Civilization*. [Online]. Available from:

  https://www.ancient.eu/Inca_Civilization/. Accessed 20 September 2017.

- D'Altroy, Professor Terence N. *The Incas: Inside and American Empire*. Audio book and course guide. 2004. Recorded Books, LLC. (Various lectures from this resource have been used throughout the following chapters.)

Chapter 1:

- First People Website. *Viracocha and the Coming of the Incas*. [Online]. Available from: https://www.bibliotecapleyades.net/arqueologia/viracocha01.htm Accessed 3 October 2017.

- Cartwright, Mark. *Viracocha*. [Online]. Available from:

- https://www.ancient.eu/Viracocha/. Accessed 25 September 2017.

- Minster, Cristopher. *Viracocha and the Legendary Origins of the Inca*. 2006. [Online]. Available from: https://www.thoughtco.com/viracocha-and-legendary-origins-of-inca-2136321 Accessed October 15, 2017

Chapter 3:

- Benjamin S. Orlove et al. *Forecasting Andean rainfall and crop yield from the influence of El Niño on Pleiades visibility*. 2000. [Online]. Available from: http://www.nature.com/nature/journal/v403/n6765/full/403068a0.html?foxtrotcallback=true Accessed October 15, 2017

- Minster, Cristipher. *The Dark Constellations of the Inca Empire.* 2017. [Online]. Available from: https://www.thoughtco.com/inca-star-worship-and-constellations-2136315 Accessed October 12, 2017.

- Urton, Gary. *Animals and Astronomy in the Quechua Universe.* Proceedings from the American Philosophical Society (Vol. 125, No. 2). 1981. [Online] Available from: http://fcaglp.fcaglp.unlp.edu.ar/~sixto/arqueo/curso/Urton%20-%20Animals%20and%20Astronomy%20in%20the%20Quechua%20Universe.pdf Accessed October 5, 2017.

Chapter 4:

- Encyclopaedia Britannica. *Andean Civilizations.* [Online]. Available from: https://www.britannica.com/topic/pre-Columbian-civilizations/Andean-civilization#ref583694 Accessed October 15, 2017.

- Encyclopaedia Britannica. *Inca People.* [Online]. Available from:

  https://www.britannica.com/topic/Inca#ref5926 Accessed October 15, 2017.

- Foerster, Brien. *Inca Rule: A Brief Timeline From Rise To Ruin Of A Great Civilization.* [Online]. Available from: https://hiddenincatours.com/inca-rule-a-brief-timeline-from-rise-to-ruin-of-a-great-civilization/ Accessed October 5, 2017.

Chapter 6:

- *The Secrets Of The Incas - Part 1 of 2.* Timeline: World History Documentaries. [Online]. Available from: https://www.youtube.com/watch?v=oRSTy9ir6zs Accessed October 5, 2017

- *The Secrets Of The Incas - Part 2 of 2.* Timeline: World History Documentaries. [Online]. Available from: https://www.youtube.com/watch?v=Kkdj39R3bAs Accessed October 5, 2017

- Dr. Sullivan, William L. *The Secret of the Incas: Myth, Astronomy and the War Against Time.* 1997, Broadway Books.

Chapter 8:

- *Incan Women.* [Online]. Available from:

http://www2.ivcc.edu/gender2001/Incan_Women.htm Accessed October 10, 2017.

- Echegaray, Luis Olivera. *The Inca Chosen Women and the Acllahuasi.* [Online]. Available from: http://cuzcoeats.com/inca-chosen-women-acllahuasi/

- *Gender roles in Inca Society.* [Online]. Available from:

  http://kendallkpsd401.weebly.com/uploads/4/0/3/7/40379583/gender_roles_in_inca_societ y.pdf Accessed October 5, 2017.

Chapter 9:

- *The Inca Pantheoon.* [Online] Available from:

  http://www.mythicjourneys.org/bigmyth/myths/english/eng_inca_pantheon.htm   Accessed October 6, 2017

- *Inca Human Sacrifice.* [Online]. Available from: http://mayaincaaztec.com/inhusa.html Accessed October 7, 2017.

- *Inti Raymi, The Celebration of the Sun.* [Online]. Available from: http://www.discover-peru.org/inti-raymi/ Accessed October 10, 2017

Chapter 10:

- *10 Most Impressive Ancient Inca Ruins.* [Online]. Available from: http://www.touropia.com/ancient-inca-ruins/ Accessed October 17, 2017

- Reed, Drew. *Coricancha, the Incas' temple of the sun: a history of cities in 50 buildings, day 3.* The Guardian. [Online]. Available from:

  https://www.theguardian.com/cities/2015/mar/25/cusco-coricancha-temple-history-cities-50-buildings Accessed October 16, 2017.

Chapter 12:

- Minster, Christopher. *Armor and Weapons of the Spanish Conquistadors.* Thought.co. [Online]. Available from: https://www.thoughtco.com/armor-and-weapons-of-spanish-conquistadors-2136508 Accessed November 3, 2017
- D'Altroy, Professor Terence N. *Lecture 5: Inca Militarism.* The Incas: Inside and American Empire. Audio book and course guide. 2004. Recorded Books, LLC.

Preview of World War 2
A Captivating Guide from Beginning to End

Introduction

The Second World War was one of the most traumatic events in human history. Across the world, existing conflicts became connected, entangling nations in a vast web of violence. It was fought on land, sea, and air, touching every inhabited continent. Over 55 million people died, some of them combatants, some civilians caught up in the violence, and some murdered by their own governments.

It was the war that unleashed the Holocaust and the atomic bomb upon the world. But it was also a war that featured acts of courage and self-sacrifice on every side.

The world would never be the same again.

Chapter 1 – The Rising Tide

The Second World War grew out of conflicts in two parts of the world: Europe and East Asia. Though the two would eventually become entangled, it's easier to understand the causes of the war by looking at them separately.

Europe's problems were rooted in centuries of competition between powerful nations crammed together on a small and densely populated continent. Most of the world's toughest, most stubborn, and most ambitious kids were crammed together in a single small playground. Conflict was all but inevitable.

The most recent large European conflict had been the First World War. This was the first industrialized war, a hugely traumatic event for all the participants. In the aftermath, Germany was severely punished for its aggression by the victorious Allied powers. The remains of the Austro-Hungarian empire fell apart, creating instability in the east. And the Russian Empire, whose government had been overthrown during the turmoil of the war, became the Union of Soviet Socialist Republics (USSR), the first global power to adopt the new ideology of communism.

From this situation of instability, a new form of politics emerged. Across Europe, extreme right-wing parties adopted ultra-nationalistic views. Many of them incorporated ideas of racial superiority. Most were strongly influenced by the fear of communism. All relied on scapegoating outsiders to make themselves more powerful.

The first to reach prominence was the Fascist Party in Italy under Benito Mussolini. Mussolini was a veteran soldier, gifted orator, and skilled administrator. He rallied disenchanted left-wingers and those who felt put down by corrupt politicians and forceful trade unions. Using a mixture of persuasion and intimidation, he won the 1922 election and became prime minister. Through a series of laws, he turned his country into a one-party dictatorship. Most of his achievements were domestic, bringing order and efficiency at the price of freedom, but he also had ambitions abroad. He wanted Italy to be a colonial power like Britain or France, and so in 1935-6 his forces conquered Abyssinia.

Mussolini was surpassed in almost every way by the man who reached power in Germany a decade later—Adolph Hitler. A decorated veteran of the First World War, Hitler was embittered at the Versailles Treaty, which imposed crushing restrictions upon Germany in the aftermath of the war. He developed a monstrous ideology that combined racism, homophobia, and a bitter hatred of communism. Like Mussolini, he brought together oratory and street violence to seize control of Germany. Once elected chancellor in 1933, he purged all opposition and had himself made Führer, the nation's "leader" or "guide." He then escalated the rearmament of Germany, casting off the shackles of Versailles.

Hitler and Mussolini intervened in the Spanish Civil War of 1936-9. Rather than have their nations join the war, they sent parts of their armed forces to support Franco's right-wing armies, testing new military technology and tactics while ensuring the victory of a man they expected to be an ally—a man who would in fact keep his nation out of the coming war for Europe.

Meanwhile, Hitler was playing a game of chicken with the other European powers. In March 1936, he occupied the Rhineland, a part of Germany that had been demilitarized after the war. Two years later, he annexed his own homeland of Austria, with its large German-speaking population. He occupied parts of Czechoslovakia that fall and finished the job off the following spring. At every turn, the rest of Europe backed down rather than go to war to protect less powerful nations.

Meanwhile, in Asia, the Chinese revolutions of 1911 and 1913, along with the Chinese Civil War that broke out in 1927, had triggered a parallel period of instability. Nationalists and communists battled for control of a vast nation, destroying the regional balance of power.

Japan was a nation on the rise. Economic growth had created a sense of ambition which had then been threatened by a downturn in the 1930s. Interventions by Western powers, including their colonies in Asia and a restrictive naval treaty of 1930, embittered many in Japan, who saw the Europeans and Americans as colonialist outsiders meddling in their part of the world.

The Japanese began a period of expansion, looking to increase their political dominance and their control of valuable raw resources. They invaded Chinese Manchuria in 1931 and from then on kept encroaching on Chinese territory. At last, in 1937, the Chinese nationalist leader Chiang Kai-Shek gave up on his previous policy of giving ground to buy himself time. A minor skirmish escalated into the Second Sino-Japanese War.

From an Asian point of view, the war had already begun. But it would be Hitler who pushed Europe over the brink and gave the war its Western start date of 1939.

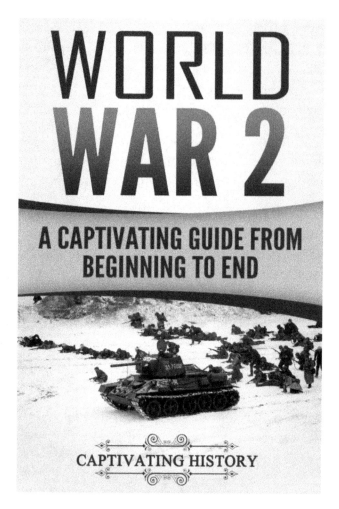

Check out this book!

A Captivating Guide to Korean War History

Introduction

The narrative of the Korean War in the West, and particularly in the United States, tells the tale of a conflict between two global superpowers and competing ideologies in a far-flung corner of the globe.

The reality is that the wheels of motion that drove the country to war in 1950 began turning long before American boots set foot on Korean soil. The heart of the conflict was a civil war between a population arbitrarily divided by colonization and the global geopolitics at the end of the Second World War.

Challenging the widely perpetuated Western narrative and getting to the core of the Korean conflict is no easy feat. From assumptions that the outbreak of war was a deliberate act of communist aggression, to the notion that Eisenhower and Truman's constant threats of atomic annihilation broke the Chinese and North Korean spirit and led to the signing of the armistice, everything needs to be dissected and reviewed on its own factual merit to fully understand the nature of the war.

This guide seeks to pull this narrative curtain and peek behind at the truth of the matter, tracing the history of the war back to the Japanese occupation and uncovering the root of Korean nationalism that stirred the nation into the frenzy of civil war in 1950.

It is about an often-forgotten war, fighting for its place in history between the two behemoths of the Second World War and the Vietnam War, which was no less significant, no less destructive, and had no less impact on the global politics of the twentieth century.

Four Maps of the Korean War

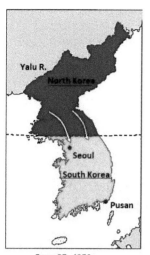

June 25, 1950

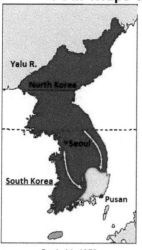

Sept. 14, 1950

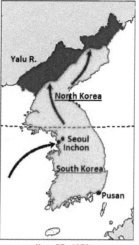

Nov. 25, 1950

July 27, 1953

Chapter 1 – The Japanese Ascendency: 1910-1945

The chain of events that brought the Korean peninsula to the outbreak of war in 1950 can be traced back to almost half a century before, at the beginning of the Japanese occupation of the country. The Korean nation, with a shared culture, language, ethnicity and heritage, deteriorated from harmonious social cohesion to a bloody civil war in just 40 years. The scars of the conflict are still etched on the Korean political landscape today. The North has a reclusive communist government, while the South has flourished as a democratic republic.

To understand the rapid deterioration and ultimate segregation of the peninsula, we must examine the conditions of the Japanese occupation of the country. Koreans under Japanese rule were a systematically divided and oppressed population. They saw their culture suppressed and their workforce mobilized to feed Japanese mouths and drive the Japanese war machine. But the period also gave birth to the Korean independence movement and began to shape Korean nationalism. Nationalist ideas would begin to be formed, both within Korea itself, across the Yalu River in China, and within the Soviet Union by those in exile. These same ideas which were bred under Japanese rule are those that gave the peninsula the political divide we can still see today.

The Japan-Korea Annexation Treaty of 1910

After formally becoming a Japanese protectorate in 1905 and handing over control of administrative affairs to the Japanese in 1907, Japanese Resident General Count Terauchi Masatake drew up the Japan-Korea Annexation Treaty in 1910, to formally transfer the governance of Korea to the Emperor of Japan. When presented with the treaty, Emperor Sunjong of Korea had no intention of signing it. But, with the ominous threat of Japanese invasion looming if he didn't, he reluctantly placed his national seal of the Korean Empire on the treaty and, rather than sign it himself, presented Prime Minister Lee Wan-yong with the document to sign[i].

Sunjong faced the dilemma of either signing the document and accepting Japanese rule, or resist and be taken by force, which would undoubtedly have left many casualties and led to a more submissive relationship under the Japanese government. The fact the Emperor himself didn't actually sign the document, and the conditions of duress that the document was presented under, has led many subsequent governments of both South and North Korea to question the legality of the treaty.

Life under Japanese rule

Despite the Emperor's seal, the Koreans were treated as conquered people. The Japanese implemented their version of military rule, known as *budan seiji*[ii]. The military and police extended their control into every aspect of Korean life. Koreans were not allowed to publish their own newspapers or organize their own political groups[iii], nor were they included in high levels of government administration. Korean land was frequently confiscated by the Japanese and redistributed.

Economically, the Japanese implemented a system of protectionist capitalism. They used Korean labor to drive Japanese industries. Koreans found themselves working in Japanese-owned firms. Any profits were sent back to Japan[iv] and only a very small and select group of Korean elites became successful under Japanese rule. In 1942, Korean entrepreneurs owned just 1.5% of the total capital invested in Korean industries and they were charged interest rates up to 25% higher than their Japanese counterparts[v]. These conditions made it impossible for the Korean working class to improve their lot and eroded the wealth of the already established middle class.

The Japanese occupiers wanted to ensure total stability and control on the peninsula, which would provide a buffer area between them and Chinese aggression[vi]. Their intention was to use the Korean peninsula to expand into northeast China and take the Chinese region of Manchuria.

They used Korea to fill a grain shortage in Japan. Rice and soybeans were exported from Korea to Osaka, Yokohama, and Yagasaki[vii]. As more and more grain left the country to feed the Japanese occupiers, there was less to go around for the Korean population. Between 1932 and 1936, the rice consumption per capita in Korea was half of what it had been from 1912 to 1916[viii].

The March First Movement

But the Koreans, who had been used to self-rule within the Chinese Orbit and were proud of their cultural traditions, were a cohesive social society. A resistance movement had been forming throughout the first decade of Japanese rule and on 1 March, 1919, 33 activists publicly read a Korean Declaration of Independence in Seoul and aired their complaints on the radio and in the newspapers.

Public protests spread across the country that day and Japanese forces responded with bloodshed and violence. Korean sources claim 7,509 people were killed by Japanese military forces, while Japanese officials are adamant the figure is lower, at 553 people. The protests were suppressed through the military, but the Korean population had made a prominent statement.

The second phase of the Japanese Occupation

In the wake of the demonstrations, the Japanese occupation under Admiral Saito Makoto entered a new phase. Unlike the iron-fisted military rule of his predecessor, Makoto ushered in a period of cultural rule (*bunka seiji*)[ix]. The strict controls on Korean culture were eased, Koreans could publish their own newspapers and laws against public expression and gathering were lifted.

But the changes were short lived. In the 1930s, the military took control of the Japanese government and the Korean colony was required to play a more important role in forging a

Japanese Empire. The Japanese launched their campaign into China in 1931, taking Manchuria and creating the Japanese state of Manchukuo. It was at this point the Japanese adopted a policy of assimilation towards the Korean population. Worship at Shinto Shrines became mandatory[x] and Korean families were forced to take Japanese family names. Korean schools were forbidden from using the Korean language and all education was given in Japanese.

In 1937, Japan embarked on the second Sino-Japanese War against China. The whole of the Japanese Empire was placed on war footing, including the Korean population. The Korean economy was modified to support the war effort. Heavy industries were introduced, with the construction of large scale chemical and electrical plants[xi]. The transportation systems were modified to cater for the distribution of resources and troops to Manchukuo, to the north of the peninsula. Although the profits were still being funneled back to Japan, the Sino-Japanese war was a period of intense economic development. They created Korean industries and brought the country away from merely agricultural development, which brought many benefits to the country in the years following the occupation.

The Japanese continued their efforts to strip the Korean population of any semblance of a national identity and culture and impose their own on the peninsula. By 1940, 84% of all Korean families had adopted Japanese names, only the Japanese language was spoken in schools and in public spheres, and they had shut down all Korean newspapers and media publications after the outbreak of war[xii]. But, in doing so, the Japanese had instigated a prominent Korean nationalist movement.

The Birth of Korean Nationalism

The Japanese occupation of the Korean peninsula created the perfect conditions for a resistance movement to grow. The *yangban* (landowning class) and the urban middle class, resented the Japanese occupation and the lack of opportunities it offered. While a select few Korean elites were becoming wealthy through collaboration with the Japanese occupiers, the majority were made landless and reduced to a state of poverty by Japanese rule[xiii].

During the first phase of the occupation, the nationalist movement was focused on middle-class *yangban* students. They regularly organized protests and engaged in pro-independence activities. The movement received financial backing from some political elites of the country, like Kim Song-su, a wealthy Korean entrepreneur who made his fortunes in the textile industry. But these entrepreneurs had to be careful. They were in business with the Japanese regime and any support for independence movements was risky and needed to be discrete[xiv].

In the early occupation period, nationalist movements among the poorer rural classes manifested themselves as small flare-ups of insurrections. Calling themselves the Righteous Army, their rebellions were disorganized and were easily put down by the Japanese military throughout the

1910s and 1920s. For the rural classes, these small revolts were driven more by anger over poverty and inequality than actual nationalist ideology.

Many Korean intellectuals and nationalists were living in exile in Soviet Russia and China, after fleeing Korea during its annexation. After the October Revolution in 1917 and the perpetuation of communist ideas across Asia, the appetite to form a pro-independence, communist movement in Korea grew. In 1918, in Irkutsk, Soviet Russia, the First Korean Communist Party was formed by Koreans living in exile[xv]. Although considered part of the Russian Communist Party, it was organized as the Korean Section.

In Shanghai, the center of the Chinese working class movement, Koreans living in exile formed a Provisional Government of Korea. They also embraced socialism as a solution to Korea's problems. The Provincial Government declared a ruling coalition with the newly formed *Koryo Communist Party*[xvi], led by Yi Tong-hwi, a former Korean army officer. Yi Tong-hwi and his counterparts in Russia used their ties and connections to spread their socialist agenda within the Korean peninsula.

Their effort was rewarded in 1925 when the Korean Communist Party was formed, on Korean soil[xvii]. However, maintaining a national communist party in Korea was a risky business. Their charismatic leader, Pak Hon-yong, had been in the Shanghai faction in 1921 and returned to Korea to form the Korean Communist Party, aged just 25. He was imprisoned first by the Japanese Military in 1925, shortly after the formation of the party, and spent four years in prison. In 1933, he was arrested again. This time, the Japanese systematically tortured him and kept him in isolation for the next six years, to the point that they believed him to be insane and incapable of leading a movement when they released him in 1939. But he came out and reformed the party, eventually fleeing to South Cholla to avoid re-arrest[xviii].

The Provisional Government in Shanghai were also busy making preparations to re-enter Korea. Kim Ku, a prominent figure in the Provisional Government, organized high-profile assassinations of Japanese high officials. He also met with Chinese leader Chiang Kai-shek in 1933 to secure financial aid for the nationalist cause. Ku promised that in return for financial support from the Chinese Government, the Provisional Government in exile would generate uprisings against the Japanese in Japan, Korea, and Manchuria (Manchukuo) within the next two years[xix]. While Chiang Kai-shek refused to give the desired financial support, he did begin a scheme whereby the Chinese forces would train military cadets for the Korean Provisional Government[xx]. However, the scheme was abandoned a year later, after heavy protest from Japan.

In the later part of the occupation, when the Japanese embarked on their aggressive assimilation policy, the Korean nationalist movement was forced into exile once again. It became too dangerous to remain in Korea and continue operations and surviving leaders of the movements described a time of constant police surveillance and job discrimination wherever they turned[xxi]. Many went across the border into China and joined the Provisional Government in Shanghai. Some fled across the Yalu River into Japan's newly created state of Manchukuo and embarked on guerrilla operations to undermine the Japanese occupation there. Their goal was to form a people's army in Manchukuo which, with the support of Mao Zedong and the other Chinese Communists, would reenter Korea and overthrow the Japanese government.

The period under the Japanese ascendancy shows a population with a strongly nationalist consciousness, but the extensive repressive measures in place prevented a single nationalist leader rising to the forefront of a Korean movement. There were several movements operating from abroad, and within the country, the student movement, the exiles in Soviet Russia, the exiles in China, the Righteous Army, the peasant movement, and the guerilla operations in Manchuria, but there was no single banner to unite and rally a population. As a result, the movement's effectiveness was severely limited under the Japanese occupation.

World War II

When World War II began in the Pacific in 1941, the Korean population was once again placed on war footing to support the Japanese effort. Half a million Koreans were forced into serving in the Japanese army. They did not receive equal treatment to the Japanese soldiers. The Japanese put their Korean soldiers in higher risk situations because they saw them as more expendable than their Japanese counterparts[xxii].

If war was tough on the Korean male population, it was outright torture for the female population. Some 200,000[xxiii] Korean women were forced into military brothels. Known as 'comfort women', these women were subjected to beatings, torture, and rape, and kept in conditions no better than most slaughterhouses[xxiv]. Many of the women never returned to their homes after the war. Many died during their ordeal, others died later due to the physical and psychological trauma they suffered, but also some refused to go home due to the intense feeling of shame. Today the Japanese government still refuse to acknowledge these 'comfort women' existed, despite the numerous accounts from survivors[xxv].

The Japanese Legacy

On 15 August 1945, the war ended. Japan surrendered to Allied forces and their 35-year occupation of the Korean peninsula came to an end. The Japanese left a divided Korean population with almost no middle class. A few Korean families who had collaborated with the Japanese had amassed a huge amount of wealth under the period of economic development, but the majority of the Korean population was left impoverished and without land. The blatant inequality between those who had collaborated with the Japanese and those who hadn't, left a population acutely sensitive to the injustices created under Japanese capitalism. In the wake of World War II, they hoped for an independent government which could address the issues of inequality and poverty.

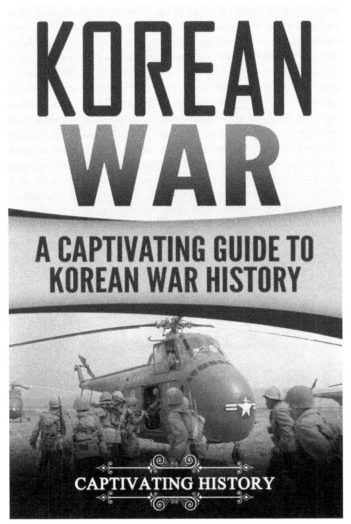

Check out this book!

Free Bonus from Captivating History (Available for a Limited time)

Hi History Lovers!

Now you have a chance to join our exclusive history list so you can get your first history ebook for free as well as discounts and a potential to get more history books for free! Simply visit the link below to join.

Captivatinghistory.com/ebook

Also, make sure to follow us on:

Twitter: @Captivhistory

Facebook: Captivating History: @captivatinghistory

Korean War Sources:

---

i Kawasaki, Yutaka. "Was the 1910 Annexation Treaty Between Korea and Japan Concluded Illegally", *Murdoch University Electronic Journal of Law*, 3,2 (1996). http://www.murdoch.edu.au/elaw/issues/v3n2/kawasaki.html. [Accessed 1 Aug 2017]

ii McNamara, Dennis L. *The Colonial Origins of Korean Enterprise: 1910-1945* (Cambridge: Cambridge University Press: 1990) p.36

iii Savada, Andrea Matles and Shaw, William. Eds. *South Korea: A Country Study* (Washington: GPO for the Library of Congress: 1990) http://countrystudies.us/south-korea/7.htm Accessed: [1 Aug 2017]

iv McNamara, Dennis L. *The Colonial Origins of Korean Enterprise: 1910-1945* (Cambridge: Cambridge University Press: 1990) p.36

v Savada, Andrea Matles and Shaw, William. Eds. *South Korea: A Country Study* (Washington: GPO for the Library of Congress: 1990) http://countrystudies.us/south-korea/7.htm Accessed: [1 Aug 2017]

vi McNamara, Dennis L. *The Colonial Origins of Korean Enterprise: 1910-1945* (Cambridge: Cambridge University Press: 1990) p.34

vii McNamara, Dennis L. *The Colonial Origins of Korean Enterprise: 1910-1945* (Cambridge: Cambridge University Press: 1990) p.36

viii Savada, Andrea Matles and Shaw, William. Eds. *South Korea: A Country Study* (Washington: GPO for the Library of Congress: 1990) http://countrystudies.us/south-korea/7.htm Accessed: [1 Aug 2017]

ix McNamara, Dennis L. *The Colonial Origins of Korean Enterprise: 1910-1945* (Cambridge: Cambridge University Press: 1990) p.36

x Savada, Andrea Matles and Shaw, William. Eds. *South Korea: A Country Study* (Washington: GPO for the Library of Congress: 1990) http://countrystudies.us/south-korea/7.htm [Accessed: 1 Aug 2017]

xi McNamara, Dennis L. *The Colonial Origins of Korean Enterprise: 1910-1945* (Cambridge: Cambridge University Press: 1990) p.36

xii Savada, Andrea Matles and Shaw, William. Eds. *South Korea: A Country Study* (Washington: GPO for the Library of Congress: 1990) http://countrystudies.us/south-korea/7.htm [Accessed: 1 Aug 2017]

xiii Pang, Kie-chung, *Landlords, Peasants and Intellectuals in Modern Korea* (Ithaka, NY: Cornell University: 2005) xiv Millet, Alan R. "The Korean People Missing in Action in the Misunderstood War, 1845-1954" in Stueck, Wiliam, ed. *The Korean War in World History* (Kentucky: University Press of Kentucky: 2004) p.13

xv Ibid. P.17

xvi Ibid.

xvii Ibid. P.18

xviii Ibid

xix Liu, Xiaoyuan, "Sino-American Diplomacy over Korea During World War II" in *The Journal of American-East Asian Relations*, 1, 2 (1992) p.233

xx Ibid

xxi Millet, Alan R. "The Korean People Missing in Action in the Misunderstood War, 1845-1954" in Stueck, Wiliam, ed. *The Korean War in World History* (Kentucky: University Press of Kentucky: 2004) p.17

xxii Daws, Gavan, *Prisoners of the Japanese: POWs of World War II in the Pacific* (New York: W. Morrow: 1994)

xxiii Shoten, Iwanami, *Comfort Women: Sexual Slavery in Japanese Military During World War II*, (New York: Columbia University Press: 2000)

xxiv Williamson, Lucy, 'Comfort Women: South Korea's Survivors of Japanese Brothels', *BBC News*, 2013, http://www.bbc.com/news/magazine-22680705, [Accessed 3 Aug, 2017]

xxv Ibid.

ABOUT CAPTIVATING HISTORY

A lot of history books just contain dry facts that will eventually bore the reader. That's why Captivating History was created. Now you can enjoy history books that will mesmerize you. But be careful though, hours can fly by, and before you know it; you're up reading way past bedtime.

Get your first history book for free here:
http://www.captivatinghistory.com/ebook

Make sure to follow us on Twitter: @CaptivHistory
and Facebook: www.facebook.com/captivatinghistory so you can get all of our updates!

CPSIA information can be obtained
at www.ICGtesting.com
Printed in the USA
LVHW110813230122
709139LV00016B/1181